Snowshoes &

SPOTTED DICK

Snowshoes &

SPOTTED DICK

Letters from a
wilderness
dweller

CHRIS
CZAJKOWSKI

HARBOUR PUBLISHING

Published by
Harbour Publishing Co. Ltd., P.O. Box 219, Madeira Park, BC V0N 2H0
www.harbourpublishing.com

Edited by Mary Schendlinger
Page design by Martin Nichols
Cover design by Martin Nichols and Roger Handling
Cover photo by Rosemary Neads
Printed and bound in Canada

Harbour Publishing acknowledges the financial support from the Government of Canada through the Book Publishing Industry Development Program (BPIDP) and the Canada Council for the Arts, and the Province of British Columbia through the British Columbia Arts Council, for its publishing activities.

THE CANADA COUNCIL | LE CONSEIL DES ARTS
FOR THE ARTS | DU CANADA
SINCE 1957 | DEPUIS 1957

National Library of Canada Cataloguing in Publication Data

Czajkowski, Chris
   Snowshoes and Spotted Dick: letters from a wilderness dweller /
   Chris Czajkowski.

Includes index.
ISBN 1-55017-279-4

   1. Czajkowski, Chris. 2. Wilderness areas—British Columbia. 3. Log cabins—British Columbia—Design and construction. 4. Frontier and pioneer life—British Columbia. I. Title.
FC3828.1.C93A3 2003   971.1   C2003-910307-2
F1088.C97A3 2003

For Nick Berwian
to whom these letters
were written

CONTENTS

I live twenty kilometres, as the raven flies, from the nearest road and neighbour. My cabins sit on a high-altitude lake in the Coast Range of British Columbia, approximately 300 km north of Vancouver. The area around the cabins boasts little human history, so its features are largely unnamed; because of a recent surge of interest in the region, however, it has now been dubbed the Charlotte Alplands after the large lake to the east. Its western boundary is the southern tip of the Tweedsmuir Provincial Park.

The Charlotte Alplands is a country of wide alpine plateaus smoothed by a very early ice age and cut by high, shallow valleys. Its most unusual feature is its plethora of high-altitude lakes. Every valley boasts three or four of them, many of them above the treeline. In the late 1980s, I staked a claim for a small fly-in ecotourism business upon the shores of a body of water almost 1 km wide and 2.5 km long. At an altitude of 1,600 m, it was only 300 m below the treeline. Working completely alone in ground too rocky for a wheelbarrow, I felled trees, man-hauled them to the site, and eventually built two small cabins. These humble structures formed the proud nucleus of the *Nuk Tessli Alpine Experience* and my ecotourism business was launched.

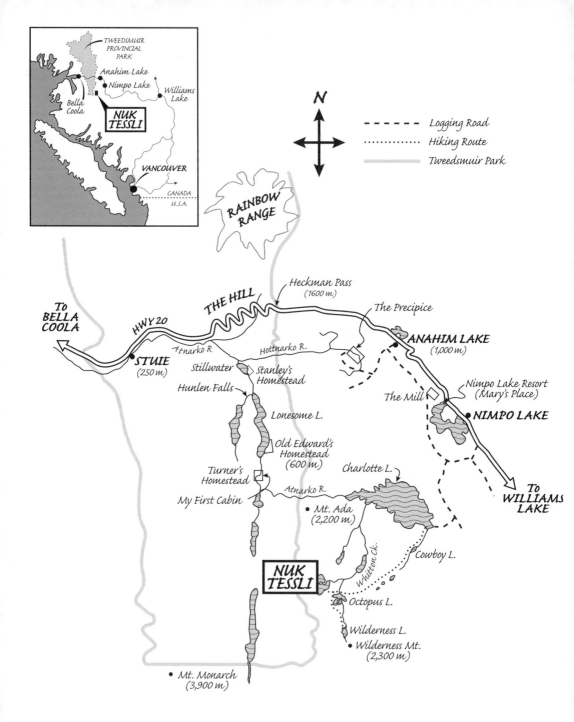

TWEEDSMUIR
PROVINCIAL
PARK

Anahim Lake
Nimpo Lake
Williams
Lake

Bella
Coola

**NUK
TESSLI**

VANCOUVER

CANADA
U.S.A.

N

Logging Road
⋯⋯⋯⋯ Hiking Route
Tweedsmuir Park

RAINBOW
RANGE

Heckman Pass
(1600 m)

THE HILL

The Precipice

To
BELLA
COOLA

HWY 20

ANAHIM LAKE
(1,000 m)

Atnarko R.

Hottnarko R.

STUIE
(250 m)

Stillwater

Stanley's
Homestead

Nimpo Lake Resort
(Mary's Place)

The Mill

NIMPO LAKE

Hunlen Falls

Lonesome L.

Old Edward's
Homestead
(600 m)

Turner's
Homestead

Charlotte L.

To
WILLIAMS
LAKE

My First Cabin

Atnarko R.

• Mt. Ada
(2,200 m)

Cowboy L.

**NUK
TESSLI**

Whitton Ck.

Octopus L.

Wilderness L.

• Wilderness Mt.
(2,300 m)

• Mt. Monarch
(3,900 m)

During those early years when visitors were few, I hiked out once a month for mail. Although the distance to the end of the nearest logging road was only 20 km on the map, the country in between was rugged and without trails. Depending on the weather and season, the journey might take anywhere from one to four days (and, on one memorable occasion during a November blizzard, six). Camps were made wherever I ended up at night. Already a veteran of the Canadian wilderness before the Nuk Tessli venture was initiated, I had discovered, some years before, the mixed benefits of enlisting pack dogs to help me carry my gear. When I was looking for a replacement for my first dog, Lonesome, friends directed me to a woman called Betty Frank. It was through Betty that I met Nick.

Betty Frank is what is known as A Character. For forty years she has controlled 600 square km of trapline and 1,500 square km of hunting territory. She talks and smokes endlessly, and hurtles through life with a momentum that lets her shrug off narrow escapes like a duck does water. She has a slim and attractive figure and is always elegantly dressed when I meet her in town, but my favourite mental picture is of her perched on the roof of her 1959 Land Rover while being driven along an execrable logging road, stripped to the skin to enjoy the first warm spring day, and yelling at her driver not to bounce so much as he was spilling her goat's milk coffee. She would have been in her sixties at the time.

Betty always had a number of willing helpers to share her exuberant life. Not just to assist with the outfitting business and trapline, but also to care for her dogs. Betty bred malamutes and huskies; she schooled them for the sled and raced them, and she used them on the trapline in winter and as pack animals when there was no snow on the ground. Sure enough, she was looking for a home for a great, woolly bear-like bitch that was no longer fertile. The dog was called Taya: she proved to be an absolute sweetie and a wonderful addition to my life.

At that time Betty's helpers were three young Germans. All were male, around twenty-one years old, all wore long hair—one had dreadlocks—and on my first visit, they were mixing a batch of multigrain dough prior to baking bread. It was the talkative one, Janis, who was doing the kneading. The quiet one in the background was Nick.

I couldn't take the dog that day but returned a couple of weeks later to fetch her. The three young men were just about to leave for a hike to one of Betty's hunting cabins at Maeford Lake. There was a logging road in there by that time and they planned to snowshoe along it, towing their supplies on a sled. When I arrived they were in the process of loading their gear onto an ordinary child's toboggan. I use kids' toboggans for hauling in the winter—they are a great deal cheaper than the fancy ones designed for backcountry skiing, and they are amazingly strong.

But mine are a solid, dark colour. The one Nick and his friends were using had yellow and pink flowers printed all over it.

Now I lived in a situation that could use such keen and energetic appreciation of the wild to great advantage. All work at Nuk Tessli was done with simple tools and muscle power: just getting the winter's firewood home was a major undertaking. Naturally I invited the young men to my place should they ever return to Canada.

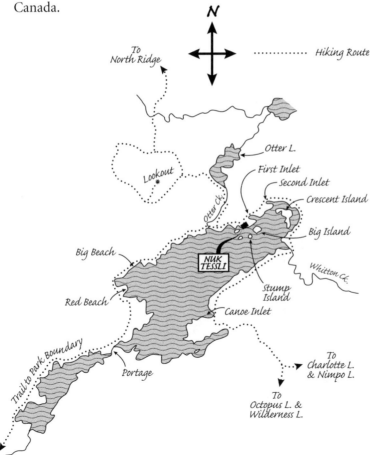

Janis and another friend, Markus, visited a couple of years later. They stayed ten days, during which they split and hauled a winter's supply of wood to the waterfront about a half a kilometre from the cabins. I later loaded it into the canoe and brought it home in stages throughout the summer. Janis and Markus's contribution was the first help I'd had with any of the heavy chores, and I loved it.

Two more years went by before Nick returned to Canada. Janis had come back with him again, and also Nick's girlfriend, Ellen. I lost no time in contacting them: would they like to come and help me build another cabin at my mountain retreat in the spring?

It was exactly the kind of thing they had hoped for. They would live in the mountains, get fed, and expend their energy on hard physical exercise. They were with me for different periods

of time throughout the spring and summer of 1998. When Nick, the last of them to leave, departed in the fall, the walls were up and the ridgepole set upon the king posts. There was still an enormous amount to do— the roof, the floors and all the interior work—and it

Janis (left) and Markus.

was natural for me to write to Nick and tell him how I was progressing (or not) without him. And because he wrote back in such a lively and literary way, the correspondence grew.

As a writer, I am comfortable with the letter format. It has a freshness not found in other forms of prose. I started my literary career by sending letters to Peter Gzowski's *Morningside* on CBC Radio and thoroughly enjoyed unburdening my soul in that way. When that outlet ceased I was bereft. Somehow "Dear Computer" did not inspire.

Then Nick came into my life. He was not only a delight to write to, he was also familiar with every facet of my existence, and the missives became detailed and expansive. I talk to myself a lot when I am alone; now my utterances could be transmogrified to the printed page, which is a much more socially acceptable form of insanity.

Thus this book was born.

A project like Nuk Tessli, created alone and with a very limited budget, is bound to acquire some eccentricities. One of mine was "spotted dick," and I soon found that I could have some fun with it. I grew up in England and was perfectly familiar with this item but most North Americans are mystified by it—particularly when told they are going to eat it for supper. Some of them have vivid imaginations...

Dave Doroghy: Nuk Tessli Guest Book, 1998

References throughout the text, in particular the quotes from my guest book that appear at the head of each letter, give clues to the identity of spotted dick. For those who cannot wait to find out what it is, a recipe is given on p. 295.

*U*sers of Crown Land in British Columbia are obliged to negotiate an agreement, through the intermediary of what is now called the Ministry of Water, Land and Air Protection, with Her Majesty the Queen. An applicant must have a commercial reason for being interested in the birds and the bees; communing with nature is not deemed sufficient. The only commercial venture to which both the landscape and I are suited is ecotourism: hiking, backpacking and nature watching. The proposal I sent in to the Land Office detailed the construction of two cabins; I would live in one and guests could either rent the other cabin and do their own thing or hire me as a guide. I would be offering solitude: I figured there must be plenty of people out there who didn't want to go to a twenty-cabin minisuburbia, with boat motors and generators and minimotorbikes and lawn mowers and portable televisions and six-packs and lumbering fifth-wheels blocking the view. Or even a less motorized ecofactory where herds of people are processed over an obstacle course like widgets. I planned to cater to an absolute maximum of six paying guests at a time. I would offer a taste of real wilderness: roadless, uncluttered and peaceful. That, at least, was how I imagined it.

I called my business *The Nuk Tessli Alpine Experience, nuk tessli* being Carrier for "west wind." The name is a reminder that I am here on sufferance only. Exploding through a narrow gap in the 4,000 m barrier of the Coast Range to the west, then screaming up 5 km of water (there is another large lake immediately above mine), *nuk tessli* gives me repeated warnings that my existence here is begrudged, that I am puny and alien: in this corner of the universe it is *nuk tessli* who reigns supreme—no matter what Her Majesty might think.

City folk may have trouble imagining a life like mine, but to me the decision to live this way has never seemed remarkable. I have never lived in a town or city. As a child I was strong and good with my hands, was intrigued and not unduly frightened by nature, was a prodigious walker, and enjoyed being alone. In my twenties I acquired mountain skills and an ability to recognize what was really necessary in life as I backpacked around the world. Perhaps my greatest fortune, however, was that I had never been programmed to think like a suburban North American. The soap-opera delivery of news, and the push-button power, water, entertainment and waste disposal that most westerners cannot imagine living without, had never been an integral part of my life. When the opportunity to build a cabin in the wilderness came along, therefore, it simply never crossed my mind that I "ought" to be doing anything else. It was only much later, when people kept asking me *Why*, that I came to realize that I might be doing something unusual. I still find it impossible to make people understand that I'm not brave or courageous or in any way extraordinary. I am just being me.

I did not come to Nuk Tessli completely green about the ways of the wild. I had already built a cabin on a property belonging to Trudy and Jack Turner, about 100 km up the Atnarko River from Bella Coola. This was also a long walk from the nearest road. As a young woman, Trudy had staked a claim 3 km above her father's homestead on Lonesome Lake; some years later (after she had married Jack Turner), the boundary of the Tweedsmuir Provincial Park was extended south, completely enclosing their quarter-section. I got to know the Turners through a mutual friend and, after I had visited them and announced my desire to live in the wilderness, they offered me a place to build.

Lonesome Lake is not far from Nuk Tessli, but it is in a very different ecosystem. It is much lower, warmer and wetter, and in a deep, narrow valley filled with giant cedars and Douglas firs that tower over the buildings. When I went there I had no idea how I was going to manoeuvre the logs but figured there must be a way, otherwise the Turners could not have erected their own structures. At Lonesome Lake, some of that work was done by horses, but I learned many tricks with levers and pulleys that later proved invaluable at Nuk Tessli. It was at Lonesome Lake that I first started pouring my heart out to Peter Gzowski on CBC Radio; these letters were afterwards expanded into my first book: *Cabin at Singing River.*

The Turners decided to sell, and they moved down into the Bella Coola Valley. Their property was bought by the Tweedsmuir Provincial Park; I might have been able to negotiate with Parks and stay there, but I yearned for a sunnier location so made a two-and-a-half-day trek through wild and trackless country further along the valley and up over its eastern rim to a high-altitude lake I had often looked at on the map. The forest was scrubby dry pine; the location had good views and good sun exposure; it was also far from any road and neighbour. It was, I decided, just what I was looking for.

Even if horses could have been brought in to Nuk Tessli, the ground would have been too rugged for them to work on. Thanks to the skills I had acquired at Lonesome Lake, however, the building part of the operation was not all that difficult. Logs were hauled with a peavey and a come-along, and raised with blocks and tackle. Materials I could not make—food, tools, hardware, steel roofing—were flown in by chartered float plane from Nimpo Lake, 35 air-km north. The Turners' property near Lonesome Lake was 4 km from the nearest place a plane could land. There, every last nut and bolt, bag of flour, toilet roll and library book had to be packed by man or beast for an hour over a rough mountain trail. At Nuk Tessli, deliveries could be made right to the door.

Finding, preparing and bringing home building materials from the forest, however, took an enormous amount of energy and time. After ten years at Nuk Tessli, my body was beginning to send out signals that such heavy physical labour was not going to be tolerated as easily as it once was. So when I started to think about putting up a third cabin, I was reluctant to tackle it on my own.

The first cabin at Nuk Tessli, the smaller one that would eventually become a guest cabin, was started at the end of June 1988. I hiked in from the road in time to meet the float plane company's Beaver loaded with supplies, and made that irretrievable first chainsaw cut into the virgin forest the following day. By the end of the summer, I had completed a log-walled shell, roofed all but the porch, and just tacked in the first windows, when *nuk tessli* decided I had been much too complacent and conjured up a tremendous storm. I huddled in my sleeping bag on the sawdust-strewn floor of the building (my tent was in shreds) through three long, maniacal days and nights, desperately wondering whether I, my building or my dream would survive. It was the noise that was the worst: the high-pitched screaming as the wind smashed into the trees after its uninterrupted careen down the lakes, and the visceral booming as it flexed the metal of the new roof like a thunder effect in a play. Twelve trees blew down in that storm. According to the radio report, it was the worst wind for seventy years in northern British Columbia. Several more storms were to beat and pummel that cabin during the subsequent winter. Although the building seemed to survive each onslaught without any ill effects, the same could not be said about me: the emotional battering was more than I could handle. So instead of placing the second cabin, the one I intended to use as a home, on the end of the point, where it would have a panoramic view, I tucked it into a little hollow at the edge of my meagre land allowance. The sheltered site worked fine as far as the west winds were concerned, but the view up the lake was compromised. In summer, the very tops of the highest mountains could be seen, but in winter, when the snow dumped off the roof on that side of the cabin, it soon piled far above the eaves.

The *Nuk Tessli Alpine Experience* staggered on in fits and starts, but it soon became apparent that my little bit of heaven was never going to pay the bills. Even one large party a year would make a considerable difference to my income. Tour groups who might be interested in what I had to offer, however, needed a ten- or twelve-client set-up to bite. A single six-berth cabin was not enough. Also, despite the availability of that cabin from mid-June to the end of September, everyone always wanted

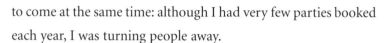
to come at the same time: although I had very few parties booked each year, I was turning people away.

Added to the tourism deficits of the situation were those of the buildings themselves. While perfectly comfortable for short-term stays, as residences they had certain disadvantages, not the least of which, as far as I was concerned, was that the windows facing the principal view were blocked by drifted snow for several months of the year. In winter, the only way I could see the mountains painted by the spectacular sunrises for which *The Nuk Tessli Alpine Experience* is famous, was to bundle up at dawn and hike out onto the frozen lake. I am an early riser and I love the drama of increasing light and the promise it brings: for me it is the most meaningful part of the day. Perhaps it was a sign of advancing age that I wanted to be able to enjoy it on occasion from the comfort of a heated room.

As the roofs stayed on and the buildings took *nuk tessli's* repeated onslaughts with no ill effects, I began to think again about the knoll I had originally chosen for my dwelling. Having an extra building on the place so that I could have two cabins for rent would certainly expand the potential of the business, and I could build a home that was better winterized, one with double-glazed windows and an insulated floor. This site would be more exposed to the wind than that of Cabin Two, but the absolute worst gusts, the ones that barrelled through the pass south of

Mount Monarch at the tip of the Tweedsmuir Provincial Park, were blocked by an island, a group of trees and a massive pile of boulders. I examined the way in which the wind swirled the snow round the boulders in winter, and stood there on calm, breathless mornings while the sunrise painted the mountains pink, orange and yellow, and dreamed dreams.

My relationship with cabin building is complex; I don't fully understand it myself. Most of the time I hate it. And yet I have spent sixteen years of my life doing it. True, it is a means to an end: I get to live in a fabulous place that for whatever reason satisfies my soul. And I could certainly never afford to pay anyone to do the work for me. But why, after the first cabin at Lonesome Lake, when I vowed: Never again! did I start the second two at

Nuk Tessli? I swore off building for life after they were completed, as well. Yet here I was considering enslaving myself with another back-breaking, misery-making, interminable project. I was dealing with menopause and was beset by a host of aches and pains that didn't seem to want to go away. On top of which, I am by nature a lazy person, and would much rather spend my time in a pleasant blur of reading, writing, printmaking, hiking and wilderness watching.

But life throws out chances once in a while. Talented, young muscle power with wilderness ideal meets middle-aged lady with opportunity. When Nick and his friends came into my life, Nuk Tessli's Cabin Three suddenly jumped into focus.

In all my time at Nuk Tessli I had yet to witness the drama of winter turning into spring. I was always out at work during those months, tree planting in the early years until my knees gave out and later doing book tours and craft fairs or whatever job came to hand. Spring is a time of year that I love. Everything is poised at the brink of an explosion of life. Down at Nimpo, that means mud for three months, but up here, the hot sun, the sparkling snow, the glorious sunrises and the long, magical—and bugless—evenings are pure heaven.

Nick, Janis and Ellen flew in at the beginning of April, just before the ice started to go at Nimpo, which meant there would be no way to get in and out of Nuk Tessli for the next several weeks except by helicopter or, with great difficulty, on foot. Janis was somewhat disappointed to find that he was not throwing logs together right away, and I had unintentionally misled him when I had talked about building a cabin, for I was well aware that actual construction would not start for quite a while. All the Germans' initial time with me would involve clearing the site, and falling, peeling, and possibly hauling the logs: this last task would depend on the ice conditions.

Straight trees of the right width and height for building are at a premium this high up in the mountains, but a stand of beetle-killed lodgepole pines at the extreme northeast end of the lake held almost all the logs we would need. The only problem was, they were the best part of a kilometre from the building site. The lake surface, in winter, is rarely icy: for most of its six frozen months, at least 30 cm of snow lies over the surface. The snow's weight pushes the ice down and the water that wells up between the cracks is insulated by the snow so that a layer of liquid remains sandwiched between the snow and the ice. This water is known as overflow. In the early part of the winter, when the snow is soft, it can be a real nuisance. Skis and snowshoes sink into it, and when it is exposed to the air, it freezes instantly to whatever touches it. By late March, the crust on top of the snow is usually fairly solid and can be walked upon without any contrivances strapped to boots, but it is either coated with a thick fur of frost or slushy and melted by the sun: in both instances, manhauling is not easy. However, to my immense gratification, Janis, Nick and Ellen stuck a toboggan under both ends of each log, harnessed themselves with ropes and dragged the monsters home. Had they not been able to do so, I would have had to wait until summer and laboriously manoeuvre each log along the lake by canoe. A log is a dead weight when towed in the water and progress is infinitely slow; also, *nuk tessli* blows more frequently in summer, and such work would have to be slotted into calm spells. The cabin building would have been delayed by at least another year.

While he was back in Germany, Nick had completed a two-year apprenticeship as a carpenter, and it soon became obvious that he was at least as well experienced with a chainsaw as myself. After all these years I still hate that fearsome and noisy tool with

a passion, so I was delighted to turn its operation over to Nick. The old Husqvarna 266, which had now built three cabins, cut thousands of boards and bucked fourteen years' worth of firewood, was still going strong, but it had its problems and I had equipped myself with a brand new Husqvarna 371. It was much lighter than the old saw, but more powerful, and I expected great things from it.

Janis was anxious to gain experience with the saw, but I was hesitant to let him use it. You would never know it by the way he flings himself with enthusiasm into every physical activity, but Janis is legally blind. Since his early teens, he has had mysterious bouts of illnesses that have been undiagnosed. It was while he was staying at Betty Frank's that his vision started to deteriorate. Janis copes so well with his disabilities that few people would guess that he has any, but poor vision is dangerous

Nick

when mixed with a chainsaw. Catching the wrong part of the bar on a stick creates kickback with potentially horrific results, and knocking the chain against a rock will wreck it. However, Janis was able to get his wish when we started lumber making.

There are two species of pine tree in my area. The lodgepole is the straightest and by far the strongest, and therefore best for all structural work, but at Nuk Tessli, a high-altitude pine known as the whitebark (*Pinus albicaulis*) constitutes about half the forest. This is often a bulkier tree than the lodgepole, but it is rarely straight and very much weaker. It would, however, make great lumber.

I regretted very much having to cut down a beautiful whitebark on the cabin site but there was no alternative; it was this tree that Janis sliced into boards with the Alaskan Mill (a frame bolted onto the chainsaw bar that acts as a guide). The tree was unusually straight and free from taper for its first 5 m and the resulting boards were magnificent, being 4 cm thick and up to 40 cm wide. I earmarked them at once for the most visible part of the new cabin's floor. They were green and very heavy, but we built a rack for them where *nuk tessli* had funnelled up from the lake and scoured the rocks clean of snow: the boards would dry there beautifully.

Janis also split and stacked the otherwise unusable odds and ends from the building site for firewood. Ellen was the principal log peeler. She did a pretty good job on her knuckles, too. She never wore gloves—she didn't need to. Her fingers were always swathed in bandages.

The other big job was cleanup. It would have been simple enough to burn the brush, but a firepit would have scarred the land for centuries in this dry, slow-growing environment, and I insisted the brush be chopped up and piled near Cabin Two, where it would do duty as kindling and summer cookwood for years to come.

A couple of years previously, I had started keeping bird records for the Royal BC Museum in Victoria. Not that I am a great birder, for I am unable to identify a great number of summer and migratory species. But the more obvious ones like woodpeckers and nutcrackers and trumpeter swans are easy enough to recognize and because I can observe activity at times when few people visit the alpine, the records are of some interest.

The juncos are almost always the first migrants to turn up. They generally appear before the end of March, but usually very little else has shown by the time I leave for whatever work I might be doing in the spring. So it was very exciting for me to observe this unknown facet of Nuk Tessli's character. As the season hurtled forward, there were new species and new songs to record every day. I wore binoculars at every waking moment—even to the outhouse. In fact, the outhouse is one of the better birding places. It is doorless, and the thicket of sub-alpine firs surrounding it is a favourite feeding ground for small insect eaters like yellow, yellow-rumped and blackpoll warblers.

The most exciting wild creature to visit that spring, however, was not a bird but a wolf. I had wandered up to the building site after supper to watch the sun go down, as I often did on those long, calm, almost balmy evenings, imagining, as always, how I would place the windows to frame the very best sections of the view. Out of the corner of my eye, I saw a movement out on the ice: a pale grey dog loped between the islands. I first assumed it was Max, a rangy Akita cross I had acquired to partner Taya, but the lean legs and large, splayed feet of this animal were very un-dog-like. In any case, both Max and Taya were in the cabin porch, still chained after their supper (they tended to fight over food if I did not keep them apart). I rushed over to Cabin One to tell Ellen and Nick. The three of us stood at the edge of the lake and watched the wolf as it poked around, lay down, got up, turned around and eventually lay down again. All the while we were talking in ordinary voices and moving without any great care. The wolf kept looking at us curiously but seemed unafraid. Finally it walked behind one of the islands that surround the cabins, and disappeared from sight.

Most years there is plenty of wolf sign in the area: tracks in the winter where they often cross the head of the lake, or even, occasionally, what is left of their kills. But I have actually seen these animals perhaps a dozen times in my life so any sighting is quite an event.

The following morning I looked out of the window—and there was the wolf again. This time it was close to the cabin. I quickly secured the dogs and fetched Ellen and Nick. This time the wolf trotted to a fishing hole we had cut with a chainsaw just beyond the ring of islands that surrounds Nuk Tessli, and, to our immense surprise, the wolf started pulling at the line. Was it in the habit of raiding fishing holes? Tiring of that, it wandered out onto the lake a little further. I grabbed some dog food and walked onto the ice with the intention of putting it beside the fishing hole. But although the animal had shown no fear when we were half hidden by the trees, as soon as I stepped onto the lake it took off full speed and never came back.

April drew to its brilliant, sunny close and I heard on the radio-phone that the ice had gone out at Nimpo. The pilots would be taking the skis off their planes and exchanging them for floats. The last mail delivery I'd received was when the Germans had flown in at the beginning of the month. My lake was still as solid as a roadway. Planes have landed on and taken off from ice using floats on occasion, but it's not very good for the floats. But would my neighbour, Nick Christianson, I asked on the radiophone, be interested in giving me a mail drop?

When I first arrived at Nuk Tessli, the only way I received mail was by hiking out to the post office at the tiny roadside community of Nimpo Lake. Once a few tourists began to arrive at my place, letters came in on their planes and, in summer, the hikes to the road became less necessary. But few people visited in winter and three months was too long to go without communication, particularly when I was trying to run a tourist business. So I used to snowshoe out to the road sometime in February. Breaking trail for four days each way and camping out in the snow made these trips real endurance tests and they are not something I would like to tackle now.

Most wilderness dwellers have some kind of outside base where they can deal with mail or phone calls or accumulate equipment and supplies. I stayed with friends at first, but soon acquired too much stuff, so I rented a cabin at the Nimpo Lake Resort. Mary Kirner owns the resort, and her neighbour, Nick Christianson, has a plane. Mary collects my mail and keeps in contact with the float plane companies so she can send my letters in with anyone who comes by. But as Nimpo Nick likes any excuse to fly, he often brings in the mail himself.

Before I came to Canada, I lived in the Falkland Islands for a while. At that time, more than twenty years ago, the only organized transport between the settlements was by float plane. If no one was arriving or departing from the settlements, the plane would not land, but as he flew by, the pilot would toss the canvas mailbag onto the grass in front of the farm office. (It was advisable to write DO NOT DROP in large letters on anything breakable that was sent through the post.) Mary wouldn't be able to send any of her free-range eggs in a mail drop, but the letters should come to no harm as long as Nimpo Nick came in the morning before the surface of the ice became too slushy.

The brilliant, cloudless weather cloned itself the next day and, sure enough, nice and early, there was the buzz of Nimpo Nick's Piper Supercub. The Supercub has room for only one passenger, seated behind the pilot. Nimpo Nick apparently told his companion: "When I say toss it out, toss it out." Well, all the passenger heard was the final three words and out went the package of mail, trailing pink flagging tape, as it tumbled toward the lake. The surface was excellent for hauling, being firm but slightly melted on the top; in other words it was extremely slippery. The package of mail hit and immediately skidded swiftly across the ice. We all stood helplessly watching it while it sped right for the only flaw in the whole 2.5 km of lake—the fishing hole. It stopped less than a metre away.

Patches of bare ground began to appear. The building site caught the sun well, particularly as so many of the trees had been removed, and by shovelling snow away so that the sun could reach the ground and thaw it, we could tackle some of the necessary digging and rock moving. I had forgotten how rugged the cabin site was; in any case, I had never seen it before without the forest growing over it. Using one big, solid in-place boulder as the south corner, we found it a fairly easy job to figure out the west and north foundation rocks, although we had to dig quite a bit for the latter. The fourth corner was a little more difficult as the land fell away right there, but by supporting the logs close to it and doing some unconventional cross-bracing, we could probably make it work. German Nick's apprenticeship had involved using laser levels and building on a pre-laid concrete foundation, so the Mickey Mouse way I approached this project, using bits of knotted string and relying largely on eyeballing, was quite a novelty for him.

At last the great day came when the first foundation log was hauled into place. I was prepared to rig up my usual cumbersome scaffolds and pulleys, but before I could even get started, Ellen and Nick had simply lifted the log onto the rocks. (Janis, always the restless one, had skied out a couple of weeks before.) Ellen is only a bit of a thing—she had her twenty-first birthday while she was with me—but she is one tough young lady. Nick is average-sized and looks quite slight when clothed, but he is exceedingly muscular and strong. Nick scribed and notched the log to fit the rocks more snugly, and there it was, the beginning of Cabin Three.

But now it was time for Nick and Ellen to depart. The tree swallows were already in residence, and on the 3rd of May a rufous hummingbird buzzed by. The surface of the ice was beginning to disintegrate, and if the two Germans wanted to avoid slogging round the lake in rotten snow, they would have to set off while they could still cross it. Ellen would be going back to Germany in a week or two, but Nick planned to return to Nuk Tessli in the summer.

And so, on the morning of the 4th of May, at sunrise, the three of us shuffled cautiously over the lake. The body of the ice was strong enough, but much of the surface was a glassy skin over a boot-top depth of water. Nick and Ellen each towed a toboggan on which lay their packs, in an effort to distribute their weight. On the far shore of the lake we said our goodbyes and I headed for home, the empty toboggans grating loudly behind me in the still, mild air.

It was the last time that year that anyone walked on the ice. Ten days later, I was canoeing.

I could no longer walk on the ice, and on land, one step would be on bare rock and the next on needle-freckled snow, which might or might not hold me up, and usually collapsed just as I took my next step. Going round the lake or up to the lookout to check on the progress of any open water as it spread from the inlet at the head of the lake was therefore not worth the effort. So day after day I would scan the ice with binoculars to see if anything was happening. It is surprisingly difficult to discern objects more than a kilometre away on a flat surface. Finally there seemed to be a distant demarcation line between ice and water, but then the wind changed and dropped. Our logging operations had produced a lot of debris around the shore—needles and small twigs, sawdust and bark chips, and these had absorbed the sun's warmth and caused a major meltdown. The gaps thus made now widened, until a sinuous narrow channel of open water snaked beside the rocks. I could not wait to launch the canoe into this exciting, unfamiliar world. Ice still joined the main pack to the shore in places, but it looked about as sturdy as wet toilet paper. This was an illusion, however. It was dark with water and no more than a few centimetres thick, but the canoe crunched into it as if hitting a concrete wall. Progress called for icebreaker tactics. I shuffled as far back in the boat as I could and, with the bow in the air, paddled frantically until the canoe had overridden the ice. Then I jumped forward before the boat had a chance to slide back into the water; with luck the ice underneath would break. Several of these manoeuvrings were necessary before the connecting skeins were broken, and I didn't get very far round the shore, but the playing was fun. The water was so clean and fresh and alive after long months of frozen immobility.

The wind batted the ice back and forth for a few days. Soon the line of open water marching down the lake was easily seen and the hissing and tinkling of the disintegrating ice candles could be heard. Within the frozen pack were open pools of calm water that reflected the brilliant blue of the sky. In them, loons, mergansers and Barrow's goldeneyes were fishing. The ice movement must have been stirring up food. What a life a fish has! Go where the grub is and become someone else's meal. Then there was a lull while the wind veered to the northeast again and the ice broke into large plates that moved slowly and silently up the lake; then it backed once more and there was more jiggling and hissing, and suddenly a streak of wind-furred water appeared beyond the circle of islands that surrounds Nuk Tessli. It grew in front of my eyes and the following day, except for a few floes in one of the bays, the ice had gone. The sunshine went with it. All at once the weather was the typical early summer gloom, a tremendous contrast to the months of blinding white. The lake was dark grey and without a ripple, and I canoed right into the middle of its brand-new mirror world.

Now I could load tools into the boat and prepare and haul most of the remaining building materials. Because of the scarcity of good logs, the piece-on-piece method of building has been used at Nuk Tessli. This is essentially a post-and-beam construction where the gaps between the uprights are filled with shorter logs. It was these shorter logs, or fillers, that I needed. For Cabin One, I had used solid logs for this purpose. For Cabin Two, I had ripped the logs in half, placing the curved side out. Log interior walls are fun for a while but they are dark and busy, a pain to clean, and a terrible surface on which to hang artwork. So I figured I would use store-bought tongue-and-groove for the inside, and place a layer of fibreglass insulation in between that and the half-logs. This would cost more cash, but save a lot of trees and a great deal of cleanup. It worked up to a point. But I had made the half-logs too thin because I had taken extra boards off them, and I had not fastened them securely enough to the uprights. They shrank drastically and many of them warped. One day I read in a Lee Valley catalogue that a tree with a right-handed spiral does not warp but one with a left-handed twist does. Most builders have few spiralled trees to deal with, but here, because of the painfully slow growth rate, it is very hard to find a tree that doesn't. Sure enough, all the badly warped slabs had counter-clockwise spirals. I have since learned that it is something to do with the expansion and contraction of the fibres as the wood flexes throughout the seasons. (Does the opposite apply in the southern hemisphere, I wonder?)

We had managed to rescue a few fillers from trees that were cleared from Cabin Three's building site, and these had been peeled and stacked to dry in the wind funnel next to Janis's floor-boards. But I estimated we needed at least eighty more; in other words, I would have to find forty logs 2.7 m long, and rip them in half. Some of these could be gleaned from what was left of the beetle-killed lodgepoles we had fallen for the framing logs. Others could be taken from natural windfalls; when these are hung up on trees and rocks in the right way they do not rot for decades in this cold, dry climate. And then there were a number of weathered snags that had no doubt died in the fire that had given birth to the very stand of trees I was now cutting down. How long ago that would have been was difficult to determine. Very few of the beetle-kills used for the frame would have been as thick as 30 cm at the butt, but the growth rings were so close it was impossible to count them accurately. As far as I could esti-mate (the first sixty or seventy years were usually readable), the stand was at least 150 years old. Fire seems to deter the organisms that cause rot and the snags must have stood there all that time. The wood inside them was clean and pink and hard; the outsides had weathered to a beautiful silvery grey occasionally streaked richly with red. I imagined these in the front of the cabin, where it faces the lake and is most visible from the water. Most people like to preserve the yellowness of new-peeled logs when they build their houses. But I wanted my cabin to look as if it had been there for centuries, and considered these fire-killed snags real treasures.

The chain-tightening screw had snapped on the new saw—which I had hardly used at this point, although Nick and Janis had operated it quite a bit—so I was back to using the old 266. Very little had gone wrong with that old saw in all the years I had abused it, but it had always been terrible to start, requiring endless yanks of the cord. Now it developed the habit of stalling and refusing to go at all when the motor was hot. So I would manage a few fillers then have to do other work while the saw cooled, then start the frantic yanking again.

Gravity was a welcome aid in hauling the fillers to the waterfront. Slinging a rope around one end, I dragged them down one by one, being careful to let the cut side slither over the rocks and trees, for the weathered finish scuffed very easily. When there was no wind, I loaded about six at a time into a canoe and paddled them home. I had wedged a couple of trees horizontally on the rocks right in front of the new cabin site—these would eventually support a little wharf—and piled the fillers on top of them until I had a stack four layers high.

I also needed rafters: these were mostly green and cut from a spot straight across the lake from the cabins. I bucked them into lengths and peeled them where they lay. By now, June, the sap had risen and the bark slipped off in great banana-skin slabs. The trees were slippery with sap so slid easily over the ground into the lake. They were too long to fit inside the canoe and I towed them home slowly in rafts, half a dozen at a time, whenever the lake was calm.

The melting of the snow on the building site was delayed by the quantities of sawdust (from lumber making and ripping the fillers) that lay upon it. But finally the tumbled jumble of rocks was revealed. It was even more rugged than I remembered. A great hole appeared in the middle and a massive boulder stuck up where the porch was going to be. The boulder was going to be right in the way. I could either simply live with it, although it would take up an inordinate amount of space, or try and remove it. Above the surface of the ground the boulder was chest high and shaped like a squat pyramid. Who knew what was hidden below?

By digging around I figured that most of it was in fact visible. Even so, it was far too large to simply roll away. I later heard of a pretty drastic way to shift a big rock: build a big fire over it, keep it blazing for a couple of days, then douse the rock with water so that it explodes. But such a fire would be pretty dangerous in this dry-forested, windy spot, as well as requiring an inordinate amount of wood. And how much water would I need? I did not think a bucketful at a time packed up from the lake would be very effective. And where did one stand when tossing the water? Wouldn't the rocks explode like shrapnel? The only way I could think of to get rid of this boulder was to bury it. But digging is not the simplest of operations in this part of the world. Most of the ground that is not pure bog is nothing but piled rocks. Any gravelly soil that might fill the gaps is full of stones. So digging is a painstaking operation for which a peavey, an iron-shod pole with a hinged hook at the business end, developed primarily for rolling logs, is a useful tool. The iron tip makes a good earth-loosener as well as a lever for heaving the larger rocks out of the way. But it is not the safest of tools for this purpose, as the iron often slips on the rock, particularly the rounded-edged granite derivatives that are the primary stones of this place, and great care must be taken not to let the handle smash you in the face, or to trap a foot when the rock rolls the wrong way.

Bit by bit, I dug a cavity in front of the pyramidal boulder. But there was one rock in the bottom that obviously was not going to shift. Sometimes by banging them it is possible to hear if there are spaces around them, but this one sounded solid and dead; it must have been another monster. Would the hole be deep enough without removing it? The side of the rock destined to go down had a great protruding bulge, so I contoured the ground as best I could to fit it around the buried monster. The backside of the boulder I wanted to move was relatively flat and, if it fell right, it would make a wonderful doorstep. But if I had miscalculated, it would be a disaster. Once the boulder was in the hole, no one would ever be able to get it out again.

With the peavey and another lever made from a small tree, and a sling of ropes and the come-along, I was able to lift the edge of the boulder. I had placed smaller rocks handy and, while my weight was on the peavey, I kicked them into the gap. Not bad going for a middle-aged lady. The boulder could not fall all the way back and I could now get a better purchase and lift it a few centimetres more. Ropes could now be tied round the rock and the come-along was anchored to a tree. The come-along would not be able to take the full weight of the rock, but it all helped. Eventually the boulder was at the point where a small push would flip it over. And, with an acrid smell of burned rock, it landed almost right. The flattish surface was sloping more than I had hoped and it wobbled a little over the boulder I had been unable to remove. I might be able to improve the way it lay, but my boulder-moving ingenuity had been used up for the present and I figured I would do something else and hope that inspiration would come to me later.

The very next day, in came a plane. Mike and Cheryl Morrison live in Nanaimo but they have a cabin at Charlotte Lake at the end of the nearest road, halfway between my place and Nimpo. Cheryl and Mike originally met me because they had read one of my books and they dropped in to say hi. (This generally happens once or twice a year.) Cheryl is like me—she has problems with flying—but Mike pops by two or three times a summer. On this visit he had his stepdaughter, Tara, and Tara's boyfriend with him, and the extra muscle was invaluable to cajole the boulder to settle at a better angle. It still sloped somewhat, but if I decided not to use it as a doorstep, it would be low enough to cover with a wooden floor.

German Nick came back on the 15th of July and within a day or two the rest of the foundation logs were fitted. We levelled the corners with a translucent tube—the kind you can buy in a wine-making store—which we filled with water. For a few dollars we had a tool of great accuracy—a far cry from holding a bubble level at arm's length and squinting over it, as I had always done before, which has resulted in one end of the floor in each of my earlier cabins being higher than the other.

The easiest way to make sure the corners of a building are square is to measure the diagonals: if they are the same, the building has to be true. Nick was constantly frustrated by the obsolete measurements in which all our dimensional lumber and tools are calibrated. He had a wooden folding ruler marked in centimetres, but the only long tape I possessed was in feet. The trouble was, the diagonals were longer than the tape.

The only way we could deal with it was to hold the wooden metric rule against the end of the flexible tape. After nudging the corners back and forth with the peavey a time or two, the diagonals eventually measured 25 feet and 44 cm.

Each year I like to try and visit an area where I have not been before to study the plants. The growing season is so short that these trips have to be done within a very narrow time frame. A good part of this window was already taken up with impending visitors and the only time I had left was the third week in July, less than a week after Nick had returned.

Nick was an early riser, and now that the lake was open, his habit was to jump off the wharf every morning for a swim before breakfast. The morning that I was due to set off on my hike, he was late. I had never known him to sleep in before but had always insisted that he should work whenever he felt like it, so at first I left him to it. When he didn't turn up after the sun had climbed high, I went over to Cabin One to see if anything was wrong. "I don't feel too good," he said. He had a headache and a fever; he wanted nothing to eat, but no, he didn't want to call for a plane to go out. He didn't think it was anything serious. Naturally my hiking trip was postponed.

Later in the day, Nick Christianson flew in with a friend for a visit, and I mentioned German Nick's problem: Nimpo Nick immediately offered to fly him out, but German Nick still maintained he was fine.

By the end of the following day he was eating a little, but had started to break out in spots. "I think you've got chicken pox," I said. "I can't have," Nick replied. "I had all that stuff when I was a kid." The following day he was smothered in spots; however, he said he felt much better and I should set off on my hike.

Four days later, I came home to a silent cabin. In front of the radiophone were the instructions for phoning the float plane company, and a book I had picked up in a second-hand store. This erudite volume was *The Practical Guide to Health, A Popular Treatise on ANATOMY, PHYSIOLOGY, and HYGIENE, with a Scientific Description of Diseases, Their Causes and Treatment. Designed for Nurses and for Home Use.* It was written by Frederick M. Rossiter, "B.S., M.D., ... Member of the American Medical Association and the Chicago Medical Society. Superintendent of the North Yakima (Wash.) Sanitarium." This new, updated version had been published in 1913.

Some of the book was plain good sense: the writer advocated fresh air and exercise in the form of daily outdoor walks, and even baths, for pregnant women, at a time when these unfortunate souls were, quite literally, confined. But other treatments were pretty horrifying: notably, in the chapter entitled Diseases For Men, electric shocks for "curing" wet dreams.

The book lay open in front of the radiophone at the pages relating to chicken pox. The description of the symptoms were Nick's exactly, even to a hand-coloured photograph of the eruptions on his skin. The medical advice was sound, merely stating that there was no cure, that it was not serious, and that it would run its course with no subsequent ill effects. Unfortunately, another colour plate was displayed on the same page. Over the words "Drawn from Life" was a most lurid illustration of a man's face smothered in smallpox.

Once on his own, Nick had felt quite poorly again. He had called a float plane company on the radiophone to ask them to contact the clinic at Anahim (20 km northwest of Nimpo) and see if there might be any complications with chicken pox. About half an hour later, without any prior warning, a plane arrived: it was the owner of the float plane company. He flew Nick out to Nimpo, and his wife drove him from the float plane base to the clinic. Nick talked to a male nurse and told him he thought he had chicken pox. "You can't have," said the nurse. "There isn't any around here." "I've only been in the area a short while," Nick replied. "I was hitchhiking in other parts of BC a week ago." So the nurse looked up chicken pox in his medical book, and found that the incubation period was two weeks. He looked at Nick. "I think you have chicken pox," he said. "Here's an antibiotic, and a salve to stop the itching. That'll be $10, please."

Now, chicken pox is a virus so Nick knew the antibiotic was pointless. And when he read the instructions on the salve, it said: Do not use on open sores. Do not use in cases of chicken pox.

Nick Christianson flew him home.

The uprights running along the sides of the cabin were short enough to be lifted into place manually without much problem, but the two king posts at the ends were 5 m tall and some kind of help would be needed. For the other two cabins, working alone, I had built elaborate scaffolding that took all day to erect, although raising the log itself took only a few minutes.

But by the time the floor joists were notched onto the foundations, Janis, his brother Alexis, and Markus (who had accompanied Janis on his first visit to my place) had hiked in from the road. Nick figured that their muscle power alone would be sufficient. I designated myself as official photographer and stood back to watch the fun. Ropes were tied to the top of the post and Nick's three helpers were strategically placed to guy it. Nick himself did the lifting. Up it went, wavering prodigiously—and down it crashed. But all was not lost. Once again, in the nick of time a plane arrived. It was carrying friends of mine from Vancouver, Miriam and Len Soet, daughter Tiana and son Jordan. Len and Jordan were both hefty guys, and before they had time to say hullo they were co-opted into the operation, and the post went up without any problem. Men lift with their muscles, it would appear; women lift with their brains.

Once the corner post next to the king post had been raised, it was possible to start a section of the wall.

In Germany, working with round logs is rare. Buildings are traditionally made with squared logs and dovetailed corners, and this is what Nick had learned. Scribing, the process of marrying the bottom of a round log to the top contours of the next, was a technique Nick had never used, but one that greatly intrigued him. He was determined to scribe the fillers for the new cabin's walls.

A log (or filler) is set upon another, and a two-armed tool, very like a school mathematical compass, is run between them. The point rests upon the lower one and the pencil scribes the upper. If the tool is kept vertical (and sophisticated models have levels on them), the drawn line exactly follows the contours of the lower log. When this is done on both sides of the log, and the piece between the lines is accurately cut out, the upper log fits the lower exactly. Fibreglass insulation is stapled into the groove before the upper log is finally rolled into place, and no further chinking is needed. If it is done well—and it takes a lot of practice and considerable finesse with a chainsaw to do so—it is by far the tidiest and most efficient way of making a cabin wall.

I used this method for the cabin at Lonesome Lake but I was pretty green at that time and the cutting of my scribed lines was not very professional. Little bits of fibreglass could be seen between the joints. Up at Nuk Tessli, I decided to forgo the scribing. Not only would it save trees—scribed logs sit tighter, therefore more are needed—but it would also save time, for the scribing process is laborious work. Furthermore, the trees around Nuk Tessli were so monstrously twisted and lumpy, they would be bound to warp, and much of the scribing effort would be wasted. So Cabin One was a chinker; i.e., fibreglass was stuffed into the gaps between the logs after they were fitted and slats of wood were nailed on to hold the insulation in place. But although Cabin Three was also to be faced with half-logs, Nick was determined to fit them together properly.

I had clients to entertain as well as the Soets to visit with, so things were pretty busy for a while. The paying guests were in Cabin One and my friends were parked in tents jammed between rocks and in front of the woodshed. The Germans were camped on the wharf: their tent had to be taken down every day in case a plane came in, otherwise the wings would sweep it into the water. Fortunately the weather was gorgeous and the biting insects were minimal. We could spend every evening out of doors. The Germans took off for a few days' hiking to get away from the crowds, but they came back in time to enlist everyone's help to raise the second king post. Eight men lifted, cameras clicked and video cameras whirred. At that

time there were sixteen people on the place, which was by far the largest number that had ever stayed overnight to date.

If I worked on the cabin at all throughout the month of August it was usually out in the bush preparing more materials, or attempting to make basement walls. These were enormously frustrating, for the bottoms had to conform to the immensely rugged boulder pile on which the cabin stood. The northwest side of the cabin was at ground level (or just below in one corner), but the southeast side averaged a metre above ground, although the variation was great. Some of the boulders were used as footings for extra supports under the foundation logs: to keep the supports in place, these had to be diagonally braced both to the logs themselves and to the floor joists. Most of this work was done while sitting or kneeling on rocks and bending into body-wrenching positions, while the sawdust and chips from Nick's endeavours rained down around me.

In the middle of August, I had a commitment outside. I was to be a speaker on the new Discovery Coast ferry, which ran from Bella Coola to Port Hardy on north Vancouver Island. BC Ferries gives a speaker or craftsperson, and his or her assistant, free passage for this service. As there was no way I could have afforded to pay for this wonderful experience, I thought it a great opportunity. My "assistant," of course, would be Nick.

I hiked out alone a few days before I was due at the ferry as I wanted to make a quick trip to Williams Lake (four hours' drive east of Nimpo Lake) to buy more supplies. I dropped the freight at the float plane base, picked Nick up and we drove across the spine of the Coast Range and down the dramatic switchbacks known as The Hill, to Bella Coola. The ferry was due to leave at half past midnight, and the rain was dumping down.

The ferry has four different schedules; the shortest takes twelve hours and the longest thirty-six. We had a fourteen-hour trip down to Port Hardy, stopping for about twenty minutes at Ocean Falls just when it was starting to get light. The obliterating rain followed us all the way south.

But on the following day, we might have been on a different planet. The scenery was fantastic, the sun fabulous and the food great, and we saw killer whales. We had prolonged stops at Namu and Bella Bella, and arrived back in Bella Coola at 5:30 a.m., when it was raining again.

While I was away, another friend arrived to house- and dog-sit. Hisako is a Japanese Canadian who came here first as a winter client but who has visited several times since. What I did not tell her, until she stepped from the plane, was that she would have eight biologists staying at the cabins. Because those of us concerned with the Charlotte Alplands have protested logging proposals in the valleys between Nuk Tessli and Charlotte Lake, the government has been obliged to send in various scientists to collect data. Lake surveyors came a couple of years ago, and now we would have the biologists. (History has shown that if they contradict industry's desires, very little notice is taken of these surveys, so how much weight the biologists' efforts will carry remains to be seen.)

I had committed myself to the BC Ferry Corporation a year before and the biologists had contacted me only recently. So, much as I bewailed the fact that I could not be around while such interesting work was going on, I could do nothing to change the dates of either activity. I also was mad at missing the chance to earn some extra money, for the biologists wanted a cook.

For the previous week, they had stayed at Mary's resort at Nimpo Lake. She does a lot of catering for crews. I knew Hisako, my cabin-sitter, would not want to cook full time for eight people—she has a career of her own and comes to my place for a vacation—so the biologists tried to persuade Mary to accompany them. But Mary had her own business to run. In the end, they compromised. Mary would still do the cooking, and the biologists would hire a plane every afternoon to fly in their meals. If we timed our arrival at Mary's dock to coincide with the supper plane, we could have a free ride home.

My niece Michelle, a trainee doctor from England, was doing a practicum in Bella Coola. After our ferry ride we picked her up, crammed her into my tiny truck and drove up The Hill in time to catch the supper plane back to Nuk Tessli. The biologists had one more working day, in which we traded as much information as possible: I went with them to examine one site and watched as cores were taken from trees to determine their age. Once again it was impossible to count the outer rings, which were simply a solid mass. These trees were very stunted, perhaps 10 m tall and only 15 cm through. They had probably germinated as a result of the same fire that had blasted the northeast end of the lake, for they also appeared to be 150 years old. One would think that these scrubby specimens would not even be considered by the timber industry but anyone driving to Williams Lake will be astounded at the multiple truckloads of matchstick-sized timber that he or she will pass en route. The plywood mill alone needs ninety logging trucks a day to feed its automated maw.

That evening, two Beavers arrived to pick up all the biologists' gear. All the freight I had bought in Williams Lake, which included twenty sheets of metal roofing, was flown in on these planes at no cost to me. What a fantastic piece of timing. And the helicopter pilot who had worked with the biologists also donated four plastic-lined 44 gal jet fuel drums, with which I planned to build a float to extend the wharf.

By the time Michelle and Hisako left, I was pretty strung out. I had not had a single day to myself for two whole months. Without periodic doses of solitude, I cannot renew my inner resources. Nick had managed some alone time by going off on hikes, but he always did that when I had other visitors. A couple of short-term parties came and went and finally there were to be three days when no one else bar Nick and myself were to be around. I looked forward to being able to do some work on the cabin.

But that afternoon, a plane landed on the lake. I am no pilot, but living where small aircraft are the main means of transport has taught me something of the problems of my immediate environment. This plane landed all right, but it was doing some very odd things out on the water.

My cabins are not situated in the most convenient place for a float plane. An aircraft must land beyond the ring of islands then taxi through a channel to reach the cabins. Unless the pilot is very used to the lake, and the wind is exactly right, the plane overshoots this channel. It then has to turn on the water and retrace its steps to the gap. If the wind is severe, this might be quite difficult, for if a gust catches the wing when it is broadside, the plane might flip. Experienced pilots never have a problem with this but newcomers to the lake sometimes take a bit of time to figure out what to do. Sometimes pilots keep their noses into the wind and simply allow their aircraft to drift back until the gap is reached.

I can tell all the regular pilots by the angle they fly over the ridge between mine and the next lake, and by their behaviour on the water. I can also pick out a newcomer by the way he circles round a time or two then usually lands much further up the lake. (I say "he," for a woman pilot has yet to land at Nuk Tessli.) Some of them try to taxi through the shallow gaps between the rocks. If they are careful, they will manage it when the water is high enough, but if I see them in time, I try to wave them around to the channel.

This pilot, however, was not conforming to anyone's patterns. He had circled around a couple of times before landing, so I figured this was his first time on the lake, but once on the water, he seemed to be having a lot of trouble. He was nowhere near the channel entrance, and a strong, gusty wind was pushing him onto the rocks. He revved his motor and taxied forward, then drifted back again. It was far too windy for me to attempt to launch a canoe and help so all I could do was watch. All of a sudden, the pilot jumped out of the aircraft onto a float, grabbed the paddle that all pilots keep there, and began to skull furiously. His efforts and the wind pushed him through one of the rockier gaps, but he must have been lucky as there was no loud ding of metal hitting a boulder. He allowed the aircraft to drift beyond the cabin, then jumped in and revved the motor with the nose pointed more or less at the wharf; however, he crunched against the rocks just before it. "Water rudders are gone!" he shouted above the wind. (These are situated on the back of the floats and are for surface control only: they have nothing to do with flying the aircraft.) "You must have wondered what the heck I was doing out there! I'm Joe ——— ."

He was, he said, a television film producer. He was making a series with the emphasis on flying and the people he met in remote locations. He wanted to arrange a time for his crew to come in to film: he couldn't do any filming right now as the batteries on his camera were going. I told him he could charge them on my solar-powered electrical system if he wanted to. He at once elected to stay the night and do all his filming himself, thereby saving himself a great deal of money.

"The chainsaw will have to be shut off, though," he said. So I went and told Nick to quit and, somewhat disgruntled, he complied. (He was anxious to finish the walls before he left Nuk Tessli, and his time in Canada was running out.) Joe filmed busily for some time as I showed him around the place. At one point I explained something and then said: "I guess I should not be talking at the wrong time while you are filming." "Oh," replied Joe, "I don't have the sound on." Nick could have worked for two hours more that day.

It wasn't long before I was finding it very difficult to deal with Joe's manner. He was impatient and demanding. As an artist myself, I could understand his desire to film me within my landscape—telling stories, putting the packs on the dogs, working the chainsaw—but his irritation with me when I did not perform like a professional actor was getting a little hard to take. I believe this is fairly standard behaviour for a film director, but at least their victims are paid to accept that kind of abuse. During the remainder of that day and part of the next I spent a total of eight hours doing the man's bidding; I gave him free food and accommodation, and received not a penny in return.

This wouldn't have mattered if the experience had been fun. But I would make a comment and Joe would say: "Oh, I gotta have that on film. Do it again." Well, there was no way I could be spontaneous the second time around, particularly with that monstrous camera centimetres from my face. Joe had instructed me never to look at the camera itself. "Pretend you are talking to someone," he said. "I'll dub in an interviewer later." Telling stories to a responsive audience is one thing. But having an animated conversation that has already lost its momentum, with a tree...?

Nick got his share of unwelcome attention as well. I had woken Joe to record the famous pink sunrise on the mountains, which happened to coincide with Nick's morning dip. This was, by now, a very rapid affair. Heavy frosts had occurred since the middle of August and the water temperature had dropped considerably. Nick's plunge was generally followed by a hasty dash into the cabin, where he stood at the back of the stove and held his arms around the stovepipe to warm through. On this occasion he had pulled himself out of the water and had just struggled into his clothes when Joe came running over. "Gotta have that on film!" he said. "Do it again!"

Because of the overhanging porch, the logs that ran the length of the roof—the plate logs and the ridgepole—were the longest components of the building, and therefore the heaviest. Even Nick could not lift them without some kind of mechanical aid. I showed him a technique I had learned at Lonesome Lake. Poles were angled up against the ends of the building to make skids, and the log was snugged against their feet. Ropes fastened to the building were looped once around the log and their free ends were held by operators standing on top of the walls. With very little difficulty, the two of us rolled the heavy plate logs up the skids. The ceiling joists were in place by then and the plate logs had to be notched twelve times to fit, a very worthy exercise in scribing.

More clients arrived. I spent a day up in the mountains with them, but the following day, while they photographed the

operation, we fitted Nick's final log in place. We tied gin poles to the uprights, put the come-along on one gin pole and the block and tackle on the other, and raised the ridgepole. At the crucial point, the float plane company's familiar red Cessna 180 arrived to pick up our guests, but we could not let them go until the final picture was taken. The pilot, however, was not only happy to wait, he promptly climbed on top of the building and gave a hand as well.

And there was the frame of the cabin, its new golden logs gleaming in the September sun and the massive ridgepole finally defining its shape.

Before Nick left the area, we planned to spend a few days in the Bella Coola Valley to witness the great drama of the spawning of the salmon. Although the valley is just over the mountains from my place (less than 100 km distant), it is a whole different world. Gone are the high, dry open pine forests; instead, heavy coastal firs, cedars and hemlock crowd the precipitous fjord.

My niece, Michelle, was just finishing up her practicum at the hospital. I picked her up again and the three of us spent a couple of days at Stuie, a cluster of private properties surrounded by the Tweedsmuir Park near the bottom of The Hill. Stuie had been my outside base when I lived at Lonesome Lake and, although some of the residents had changed, I knew the area well.

Michelle had so far had a rather peculiar view of Canada compared to that of most overseas visitors. Immediately upon

German Nick and Max.

arriving in Vancouver she had caught a ferry to Vancouver Island, taken the bus to Port Hardy, then ridden the Discovery Coast ferry to Bella Coola. She had worked in the little hospital there for six weeks and, apart from the time she had spent with me and one trip to Anahim, when she accompanied the doctor on his weekly visit to the clinic, she had seen nothing of Canadian life. She had never seen a Canadian Tire or a Save-On Foods—she had never even seen a moose. She had, however, encountered eighteen bears.

The Bella Coola Valley is a haven for grizzlies. They are particularly visible in the spring and again during September and October, when the salmon are spawning. The spawning itself is an incredible sight—all those huge, distorted, rotting fish living out the final drama of their lives. Unfortunately 1998 was a disastrous year for the fish and there were hardly any in the river. I had never seen it like that before. It is very alarming when a species numbering countless millions suddenly disappears.

Near Stuie there are a number of attractive hikes; one of them follows an esker high above the river. It is a great place to look down onto the gravel bars and observe bears. On one, we saw a black grizzly sow with two cubs. (Michelle's tally was now twenty-one.) The trail leads to a campground, which, thanks to a brief opening for steelhead, was jammed with vehicles and generators that were running to operate freezers. Anglers crowded the riverbank, casting doggedly, grim expressions on their faces, to the tune of the roaring motors. People think that's fun? Past the campground another trail terminates at the confluence of the Atnarko and Talchako rivers. The first is a clearwater stream and the latter is cloudy with glacial silt; the two rivers run side by side for a while before their waters mix. Behind them, a magnificent array of mountains form a spectacular backdrop to the scene.

Just before it reaches the viewpoint, the trail parallels the river but is hidden from it by a thick wall of brush. Last year's cottonwood leaves were as crisp as cornflakes and the noise we made walking through them was so loud we had to raise our voices to speak. "We won't have any trouble with grizzlies making this racket," said Nick. At that very moment, only metres away, a young blond bear came up from the river through the barrier of brush and stared at us. (I had left my dogs chained at Stuie; bringing them into a situation like this would have been asking for trouble.) Without a pause, we turned around and started to walk back up the trail. Nick and Michelle were almost running—absolutely the wrong thing to do. But you don't have to be able to run faster than a bear when you meet him. You only have to be able to run faster than your friends. I yelled at them to slow down as I could not keep up. I glanced behind and caught the silhouette of a much larger bear behind us. It was Mama, following us along the trail. Fortunately when we veered away from the river, the bears didn't follow, but we all had a bit of a fright.

At Stuie there lives an interesting man named Ron Mayo. He has studied the bears there for generations; he knows them all by sight, and has kept records of their genealogy since he first started filming them thirty years ago. He had been out walking the river when we had arrived, but upon his return we told him of our encounter at the confluence. "Oh, that'll be Maple," said Ron. "She has two two-year-old cubs and the male is a little bit too nosy. Poor Maple has to keep after him to make sure he doesn't get into any trouble."

At the head of the valley, just before the switchbacks start to climb up the precipices toward Nimpo, a small, very rocky road runs a few kilometres south, following the Atnarko upstream. This is the Tote Road, start of the Tweedsmuir Park's hiking trail to one of the many spectacular features of the area, Hunlen Falls. But if you ignore the trail when it begins to climb the side of the valley, and continue to follow the river, you eventually arrive at Lonesome Lake: 4 km upstream from that body of water is the location of my very first cabin. To reach it, however, we would have had to hike for most of two days and we did not have the time. Instead we visited the Stillwater, the first lake upriver, and only 5 km past the end of the Tote Road. Fortunately a friend has a canoe stored there and we could borrow it to paddle up the lake. Canoeing up the Stillwater during spawning season can be an exciting experience. I have been in there some years when the salmon were so thick it was like paddling in fish. They leapt in a constant syncopated rhythm of plops and splashes and flowed past the bow through the crystal clear water like an underwater wave. This year we saw a grand total of six.

Although the salmon's non-event was disappointing, our little expedition was not completely thwarted because we had another purpose in visiting the Stillwater. Trudy Turner, whose property I built on upstream from Lonesome Lake, has two brothers. John Edwards lives on their parents' homestead at the head of Lonesome Lake, and Stanley occupies a quarter-section at the head of this one.

Ralph Edwards, their father, had been wonderfully inventive. He had constructed a wooden water wheel to drive a sawmill (having been told it could not be done), and his crowning achievement was to rebuild the body of an airplane to fit an engine that was too big for it. He originally intended to make the whole plane from scratch, and he and Trudy hauled the motor in by travois when Lonesome Lake was frozen. But the powers that be announced that they would refuse to license such a craft, so he and his family scraped together the means to buy a Taylorcraft; when its motor quit a couple of years later, Ralph replaced it with the engine he had on hand. When the plane was eventually inspected, it was pronounced structurally perfect. All of Ralph's engineering was accomplished with no specialized schooling: he learned everything he needed to know from books. Trudy, John and Stanley had all inherited their father's ingenuity.

Stanley's property was mostly swamp, but during the time I travelled up and down the Atnarko, he drained a good portion of it with a most impressive array of ditches, all dug by hand. The soil in those bottomlands had not a single stone in it and he grew the biggest vegetables I have ever seen—his radishes, which were as sweet, crisp and peppery as you could wish, were the size of my fist.

Stanley is a striking figure, tall and skinny, with a long white beard and a yellow hard hat. He often meets hikers on the trail north of the Stillwater and he takes them home and tells them stories about his encounters with animals. His friends are the bears and the grouse and the little fishes that hatch in his drainage ditches. No creature is beneath his notice: on one visit I made he was scything grass for hay, and he showed me a clump he had left because a spider was sitting on its web in the middle of it. He was going to wait until the spider had done with it before he cut the grass down.

Stanley Edwards

I had not seen Stanley for a few years. I knew he was quite deaf so was not unduly worried when there was no reply to our yells as we beached the canoe and walked up the muddy trail to the plywood shack he calls home. But his hearing must have deteriorated further for, even right outside the walls, our shouts had no effect. There was smoke coming out of the chimney so he was most likely at home. I picked my way past a huge heap of discarded Coffeemate jars and Campbell's soup tins, and banged loudly on the rickety plywood sheet that did duty as a door, opening it at the same time.

The stench that came out of that shack was appalling. To my knowledge, Stanley never bathed, and his cats had used the sawdust and garbage floor as a litter box. I used to spend the night at his place occasionally when the weather was too poor to travel, and I was always grateful for his hospitality. But I always slept in the barn.

But here was Stanley, sitting on his single chair, his lined face breaking into a delighted grin. "Chrisco!" he said in his wheezy, old man's voice. He lip-read without trouble, so as long as we faced him we could converse quite easily. He offered us coffee, which we declined, so he immediately took us on a tour of his place.

His ditch project must have been completed, for Stanley had now turned his attention to building roads. Not just one, but a veritable spaghetti junction of them. They were not built on the bottomlands where the digging was easy, however, but at the base of the steep valley walls where boulders abounded. Nonetheless, each road was graded perfectly and as smoothly as a paved highway. They could have handled an ATV with ease. Stanley's only tools were a pickaxe, a shovel, a crude homemade level and a wheelbarrow.

Our tour must have lasted a couple of hours. Stanley strode ahead at a speed that made me breathless and chatted happily about the adventures he'd had with his various wild friends. He demonstrated his prowess with balancing rock sculptures he'd made by the sides of his roads. He eventually hoped to link his network of trails to the Tote Road. He probably already had enough mileage, except that so much of it branched off to other destinations.

We could not stay longer for we needed to hike to the Tote Road before evening when the grizzlies were most likely to be active. But on our way back to the canoe we swung round by the garden and grabbed bunches of delicious, giant carrots, wishing we had brought backpacks with us so that we could take some home.

"I never thought that something called Spotted Dick could be so enjoyable. But it was."
—Glenn Griffin, Nuk Tessli guest book, 1999

15th Nov 98

Dear Nick,

That newspaper article you sent me was hilarious. Your German reporter friend must have been angling for the newspaper-writer's fiction award. No wonder you were too embarrassed to translate it for me. "All alone in the wilderness"—Hah! Instead of the photo of you working by yourself on the ridgepole, you should have given him the picture of everyone raising the second king post—when there were sixteen people staying here. Don't you remember complaining that Nuk Tessli was not isolated enough for you? And "planes might not arrive for several months"? Wasn't it you who expressed disgust during that period of three weeks or so when someone was flying in for one reason or another every single day? And what's this about never getting sick? Doesn't chicken pox count? (Admittedly, you didn't catch it on the place.) And "having to go and catch fish when you are hungry"! How many fish did you actually bring home throughout the summer? Four? My German is poor and the little dictionary I possess only had half the words in it, so I may have misread some of the article but I couldn't find a single mention of all the dumplings and spotted dick! But the most ludicrous comment had to be the one about the gun. How you "had to keep it loaded and hanging on the building at all times in case the bears came by." What bears? I don't recall seeing one anywhere near the cabins all summer. And what gun? Do you even know where I keep mine? Such ridiculous distortions that pander to a city person's ideal of the wilderness always make me mad. They perpetuate ignorance. How can people make educated decisions about the environment when they are fed that kind of garbage, and assume it to be true because it is in print? And when you see such an obvious twisting of the facts, it makes you wonder what else is so grossly misrepresented in the media.

And did you receive the video of our dear friend Joe's television show? I must confess I thought that the content actually wasn't too bad: Joe portrayed me in much the same way that I see myself, warts and all. And you did pretty well trying to be civil after your repeat morning swim. But what an amateurish production! Especially when Joe himself with his stiff, awkward smile was giving his introduction. He'd obviously simply stuck his camera on a tripod and sat in front of it. What a cheapo. No one was telling him to "do it again." It was like the worst kind of home movie. "Well, at least it's TV," you might think, "so you're getting publicity for the business." But this kind of exposure never amounts to anything as it's hitting the wrong section of the public. So far two people inquiring about bookings have mentioned that they saw the show, but both of these people already knew of me because of my books and magazine articles. Advertising works only if it is done in the right place. A very attractive article was written about me for a glossy Canadian outdoor magazine last year and I received a grand total of six letters as a result. Two were booking inquiries that never came to anything, and three were from young people looking for (paid!) work. The last came just recently: a letter from a young woman in Calgary calling herself a movie producer. Another one. She was completely unaware of Joe's efforts. She wrote in a "Guess what! I'm going to put you on TV" kind of way. She "wouldn't be any bother," she said. She "just wants to follow me around for a couple of days." Whoopee. I'm going to write and tell her my guiding and cabin-renting fees and I bet that's the last I hear from her.

The good weather we had for most of the summer ended abruptly after you left. There was fresh snow well below the tree-line to accompany me on my way home. It looked both sad and pretty against the last of the yellow leaves on the willow bushes, with the dark mountains rearing behind. The snow cover was continuous over the alpine section, and while it wasn't very deep, it was enough to slow me down so that I had to spend the night at "Chateau Bob," as one of my visitors called the old trapper's cabin near Octopus Lake. It has developed a prodigious lean and I fear one more heavy snowfall will be the end of it. It is a good job it was a dry night as I could see chips of stars through the gaps in what is left of the sod roof.

Right near there is that two-log bridge I built a number of years ago. There was no snow at that altitude, but there had

been a heavy frost overnight and the bridge was covered with ice. I decided I would rather risk wading the river, which is only ankle deep upstream of the bridge at this time of year, and by tippy-toeing and running fast I didn't get much water in my boots. But the dogs, neither of whom like water, preferred to keep their feet dry. Taya is getting old and slow, so as there was not a lot to carry, she had no pack and made it across without problem. Max stepped onto the bridge confidently enough, but halfway over, he suddenly realized he was in deep trouble. Even in October the hole directly below the bridge is large enough to drown him if he falls in with his pack on. He inched along, a terrified expression on his face; I whipped out my camera and, with luck, I will have caught him during his most anguished moment.

Putting the roof on the new cabin, at least over the main part of the building, was a priority. Without the roof, I would have no snow-free space to store things like lumber and the rest of the roofing metal, and if these things were not to hand I could do no more work on the cabin throughout the winter. But the weather that slowed my hike from the road wasn't about to let up in a hurry, and during the early part of October it did nothing but rain and snow and blow: balancing on the widely spaced boards tacked to the ceiling joists, in a howling gale, was not to be borne. I was going to need a lot of chainsawed lumber, for the gable ends among other things, so I used that bad-weather time to go into the bush with the Alaskan Mill. It is a job I absolutely loathe at the best of times. A couple of logs were down already but I found another suitable beetle-killed whitebark and managed to coax about twenty useful boards out of it. The wet snow on the ground facilitated sliding the lumber down to the waterfront, so that, at least, was a plus, and I packed them home in the canoe.

Finally the weather was dull but dry, and only moderately windy, so I could continue with the building. I did what you told me: put two-by-fours (which I made especially) on top of the ridgepole to give me something on which to notch the rafters. I

must admit, I am very impressed with the legacy you have left me! Whenever I laid the level down on the flattened top of the ridgepole, the bubble was always exactly in the middle. None of my other roofs are anything like so accurate. I really can't imagine how you calculated it all with such crude materials and tools.

It was a precarious job getting the two-by-fours on top of the ridgepole, as I was too lazy to build an elaborate platform to work on, and utilized a small table perched on the boards. But the boards were widely spaced as there were not enough to cover the whole ceiling, and one or another of the table legs was always nerve-rackingly close to a gaping hole. The two-by-fours were green and too heavy for me to lift unaided, so I resorted to my usual tricks with binder twine. I tied a string to one end, hauled it up a bit, repeated the manoeuvre at the other end, then back and forth until the timber could be nudged up top. At last the first pair of rafters, poles from the bush that had been flattened on one side to receive the strapping, could be notched on and diagonally braced for extra strength. With the way the wind pounds this location, I put in extra braces wherever I could.

It was going to be much easier to face the gable end while I could stand on the structure, rather than try to do it from a ladder once the roof was on. So, using some of my nicest new boards, I edged them with a chalkline and chainsaw and fitted them and nailed them in place. At some point I will nail battens over the gaps but they will do for now. At once I received a surprising amount of shelter from the wind, which was an unexpected bonus as it was quite bitter up there. The next couple of pairs of rafters posed little difficulty, but after that I ran into the area over the bay window. I've always wanted a bay window but I had no idea how much extra time it would take to construct one. It's almost like building an extra cabin. I remember reading somewhere, and now know it to be true, that the size of a building has only minimal effect on how long it takes to complete it. The bits that use up the time are the corners, and a room with a bay window has four more than one with straight walls. The basement took twice as long because of it, as did your work on the walls. And the roof is too steep to extend it over the bay window at the same angle, so a whole new set of rafters had to be fitted.

As soon as half the roof was raftered, I started putting on the strapping for the metal sheathing. To handle the sheets of rolled steel I would need dead calm weather and that is rare enough here at the best of times, so I wanted to be ready for them as soon as possible. The first morning I tried to put up a piece, the wind got up before I had lifted it onto the roof and the metal bowled happily along over the rocks. Fortunately it wasn't damaged, except for a few scratches. The following day, however, I got the calm spell I needed. The first pair of sheets needed a lot of adjusting to make sure they were exactly square to the roof; otherwise there would be all sorts of problems by the time I reached the other end. The wind was too strong to continue by the time those were in place, but at least I had started. Every time there was no wind, usually first thing in the morning, I sneaked up another sheet or two. The windy times were spent fitting the other rafters and the remaining strapping. I had to use some precious calm hours to go across the lake and fall and tow home more rafters. I had enough for the main part of the building but needed more for the porch. I didn't think I would have time to make the porch roof this fall, but if I had the rafters handy, I could at least continue with it during the winter. Mindful of your efforts in hauling the logs across the ice, I decided that getting the trees home in winter would be too difficult for me alone; the only practical way was to paddle them across the water while the lake was still open.

Although my lake usually stays ice-free until late November or early December, the float plane company takes its planes out of the water around the end of October, as many of the shallower bodies of water and even Nimpo Lake itself begin to freeze. Travel overland can also start to become very difficult at that time, so now I either try to hike out before Thanksgiving, when conditions are usually not too bad, or fly out just before the float plane company's deadline. But the end of October came and the roof was still not finished. The weather continued mild and dull; anxiously I watched the snow levels in the mountains. The calendar ticked over into November; flying was now out of the question, but the weather continued to co-operate. There were a few centimetres of snow on the ground when I completed the main part of the roof and battened down the place for winter. I hiked out on November 8th and 9th, in falling snow, but with no more than 30 cm to wade through in the alpine areas, and arrived at Nimpo without mishap. The weather gods, in the end, had been kind.

Love

Chris

"It's a bit rude, isn't it?"

—Sarah McLean, conversation, 1997

28th Feb 99

Dear Nick,

This winter has been very different from last year. It has not been at all cold. The thermometer never registered temperatures below –25°C and even that has not happened very often. Last year, the coldest was –50°C and we almost always have one or two spells of –40°C. But the mildness this winter has brought snow. Usually most of the snow falls during a three- or four-week spell in December or January. This year, however, it never quit. Often it is only a kind of mist snow—this happens when the cold air comes up the valley from the Chilcotin but warm clouds, visible above the mist snow, sail in overhead from the coast. These conditions sometimes persist for days. It is very frustrating when you can see the blueness in the fog overhead and it looks as though it could clear any moment and yet it never does. Accumulations with this mist snow are negligible but the northeast wind makes life uncomfortable and the gloominess is depressing at the least and frustrating when I want to spend time on the computer.* Interspersed with these periods there have also been several big dumps. When I first arrived back on Jan 2nd, 80 cm had collected around the cabins—a little heavy for Christmastime, but not unusual: now there are 180 cm, which makes it pretty close to a record. The pegs on the clothesline are touching the snow. I have done a lot of shovelling. I had visitors in Cabin One last week and before they could use it I had to dig out the chimney, which was completely buried. While they were there, the roof slid clear and the kitchen window was smothered. I never thought that window would need a shutter and it had to be dug out very carefully to avoid breaking the glass.

Nuk tessli flexed his muscles a few times at the beginning of winter and the drifting of all that loose snow was spectacular. I had thought that the new cabin had been placed to avoid the main blast of wind from the lake, but in fact it screams up the gap where we stored Janis's floorboards and clips the corner of the building, being then deflected across the end with tremendous fury. The most fantastic and beautiful snow shapes have been carved around the group of rocks in front of the cabin and yet the ground by the southeast corner has been blown bare. Tons of snow flew under the end wall where the basement wall is not yet made and smothered the pile of lumber and the last pieces of roofing metal that had been stacked on the floor joists

*The computer is operated by solar power.

last fall. Heavy tools like the peavey are also in there somewhere but completely unrecognizable under great pillows of snow. Outside, an eaves-high drift parallels the north wall of the cabin. It has developed a curving crest like a wave. Some of the storms came from the south and the gusts were so strong they shook Cabin Two, and that has never to my knowledge happened before. Perhaps the trees I cut down for the new cabin had protected me in the past from the wind in that quarter. But when Nimpo Nick and Mary flew in during a brief window of calm, they told me that tremendous windstorms had hit Vancouver and roofs had been blown off and trailers knocked over, and of course power was out for days in some places. But although the winds were noisy and inconvenient here, I was happy to see them because not only did the new cabin, roof and all, stand up to them beautifully, but also the remaining trees around it did too. I had put all kinds of extra bracing under the new roof in case of an uneven snow load—something I had not done for Cabin Two and had to try and compensate for later—but I need not have worried. The wind simply blows Cabin Three's roof clear.

Needless to say, at the leeward end of the cabin, the snow piled high. The porch ceiling joists are currently at the level of my waist—hopefully there will be the same amount of snow next year, as that will make life a great deal easier when I move house and want to load stuff into the attic.

Once in a while we'd get a bit of sunshine and I'd think: finally we are going to get a good spell. But there was rarely a single day during the first six weeks of the year when snow of some sort did not fall. It was pointless to continue working on the roof under those conditions. Instead, my main job so far during this winter has been cutting lumber. For some time now I've had my eye on a stand of good-sized, beetle-killed whitebarks beside a section of the trail that forms part of the loop to Otter Lake. They were separated from my lake by a short stretch of forest and several hundred metres of swamp, but I figured that smaller items like boards could be dragged at least as far as the waterfront on the snow, even if not all the way home. One reservation I had about using this stand was that all the trees had left-hand twists, the one most likely to warp. But the twists were only slight, and I figured that if I used screw-nails to batten the boards down, they would probably stay put. Most trees in the area turn to the right, so I assume this stand, which were all about the same size and thickness, must have been from a single genetic stock, perhaps planted from the same cone by the nutcrackers the last time a fire went through this patch. The growth rings on most of them were too close to count, but I took a thin round off the largest stump (a metre and a half above ground, as there was too much rot below that height), and by counting the first hundred rings, which were just distinguishable, and estimating the rest,

I'd guess it must have been at least four, possibly five hundred years old before it succumbed to the beetle's parasites. It measures 50 cm across. That's just slightly more than the distance between my elbow and the tips of my fingers. And the logging companies, who are panting with hot breath over the trees in the valleys close to here, are claiming that they can mow the forests down as fast as they do and maintain sustainability because the forests will be ready to cut again in another 120 years.

At first, wind and snow often prevented me from working at the lumber site, and even when the weather was not too bad, the days were so short I could manage only three or four hours' cutting time. Just getting the tools up there was a major task, for I had to break a deep trail with snowshoes a couple of days beforehand so I could pull the two toboggans I needed for the equipment along it. I packed along the mill and its tools (wrecking bar, spikes, hammer and wrench), chain oil, an old bucket of miscellaneous chainsaw tools and parts, both saws and two gas cans (each saw needs a different mix), an extra pair of snowshoes, the peavey, the snow shovel and that rickety old aluminum ladder that was given to me last summer. Falling trees in deep, soft snow is nerve-racking, as it is impossible to run away quickly and the hidden ground, as you know, is just a great uneven jumble of boulders and holes. At the beginning of winter when the snow was not so deep I would tramp round and round the tree the day before I cut it down to let the snow set up a bit; later I dug a big pit in the snow around each tree so I did not lose the metre of trunk that was buried. The four snowshoes were then spaced like stepping stones along my escape route. In these conditions, as the tree fell it completely buried itself with a great *whooomff!* and I had to shovel the snow away from it before I could even cut the

branches off. Once that was done, the snowshoes could be laid beside the log to give me a platform on which to work.

Weather delays might be frustrating but they were to be expected; however, I can never forgive a piece of machinery when it doesn't perform as it should. Last spring, when I was cutting wall pieces, I had used the new 371 for only a couple of days when the bar-tightening bolt snapped. I couldn't get a replacement until I went shopping in the middle of June. The saw worked fine all the time you were using it during the summer, but the minute I picked it up in the fall, it broke again. This time it stalled in mid-use, then simply wouldn't start. Most of the roof-building work had to be done with the old 266. Nimpo Nick flew the 371 out about two weeks before I left to go craft fairing in the fall, and Mary happened to be going to town so she took it in and got it fixed right away (the ignition had gone), but Nick could not fly it back before freeze-up because the weather was too bad. It came home with me on Jan 2nd and the first time I tried it out was on the first day of lumber making. I had put it on the mill, and was keeping the old one for bucking and limbing—it's great not to have to take the mill on and off all the time. But the newly repaired 371 ran for exactly one and a half minutes and quit again. Same thing as before: it just wouldn't start. It was two and a half weeks before Nick dropped by and I was able to give him the saw. In the meantime, I used the old saw on the mill.

It would cut two or three boards OK, but then start its stalling business. Pulling that old saw to start it is a real problem at the best of times, and it is much worse when the saw is lying on is side attached to the mill. What with the short daylight, the difficulty of simply moving around in the snow, and the necessity of waiting for the 266 to cool, I considered myself lucky if I got six boards made in one day. Then, with all the extra frustrated yanking, the cord started giving me trouble. After a dozen pulls, it would pop right out and I would have to take the side off the saw and rewind it. (This, needless to say, meant removing the mill as well, a tedious, knuckle-skinning job at the best of times and lots of fun when everything is plastered with snow.) Finally the pulley (the bit that the cord is wrapped around) broke. Part of the top had come away. Nimpo Nick had only just visited at that point so I knew it might be two or three weeks before he came back. There was half a log lying in the snow and if there was a big dump of snow before I could get back to it, it would be difficult to find. I tried gluing the pulley together with five-minute epoxy, and strengthened it with a canning jar lid stuck on top. All went well at first but after three starts, I could hear scratchy grating noises as the canning jar lid began to disintegrate, so I continued working on the log without switching the saw off at all, even when I put gas in it. Luckily it didn't stall and I was able to finish the log, but I was not able to start the saw again.

So now I had no saws at all. I phoned Nimpo Nick and asked him to get a pulley shipped out from Williams Lake on the freight truck. It was three more weeks before the weather allowed him to come in again. And when he did, the pulley was the wrong size. It looked right when held beside the broken one but unfortunately I didn't try and fit it until after Nimpo Nick had gone and then I found that the central hole was too small. Nimpo Nick had brought back the re-repaired 371, however, so later that day I broke trail again up to the logging site and with great apprehension started it up. If it didn't work, I would have another three weeks at least without any saws. The new saw worked fine through the first board. At the beginning of the second board, the bar came off. They must have taken it off in the shop and not tightened the nuts properly. Not only were the bar nuts missing (I managed to find one in the snow), but the bar tightening bolt was broken. Again. That is never supposed to happen. Well, I had the old saw to cannibalize—but its bar-tightening bolt was much shorter. When the bar on the new saw was assembled, the little nipple that holds the bolt in the groove was hanging on by a single thread.

But for all that, it worked. When Nimpo Nick came again, I sent out the broken pulley from the old saw, plus the wrong pulley, and also the broken bolt from the new saw. When the next mail came back after that, the pulley was finally right so I could put the old saw together again, but the bar-tightening bolts bore no relationship in size and shape to the one I had sent them. You wonder what some people have between the ears in these places. Not only have they wasted weeks of my time, but also the freight due to their mistakes has cost me about fifty dollars. I am going to refuse to pay the chainsaw bill unless they credit me for the cost of the freight. The faulty ignition was still on warranty so they will end up owing me money.

The first time Nimpo Nick flew in was a rare sunny day and the temperature was −25°C. I had broken fresh trail with the snowshoes after a recent fall and was hauling a load of boards on the ice. I had a number of really nice ones; using the ladder, rather than another board, as a guide made them straighter and also slightly thinner than the floorboards. They would be good for jobs like making doors and framing windows and as the snow was too deep to stack them properly in the bush (they would simply have fallen over when the snow melted and probably warped and certainly not dried), I wanted to store them under a roof. By lashing a toboggan to each end I could manage three boards at a time, or four if conditions were really good. A pretty good bobsleigh run developed in the bush as a result of all this tobogganing. Because most of the pulling on land was downhill, that part of the job was not too bad, although it involved a lot of finagling around some of the tree wells, where the load wanted to slide sideways and tip. But the snow on the lake was deep, loose and fluffy, and there were 8 cm of water between it and the ice. If the load fell off the packed trail, it flipped into the water and had to be untied and reloaded before I could continue.

It was one of those fabulous clear days that are all the more remarkable when there has been so much gloom. I heard the high buzz of Nimpo Nick's Supercub long before I saw it. I was too far from the radiophone to warn him of the conditions on the lake, so as he landed, he sank into the overflow and got his skis gobbed with frozen slush. We lifted the plane so that we could put chunks of firewood under the skis, then Nick crawled under with the axe and chipped away every scrap of ice. Otherwise he would not have been able to get up enough speed to take off. When we set the plane down again on well-tramped snow, the skis immediately froze to it. I had to grab the wing strut and rock the plane while he gunned the motor. The noise was indescribable and you can imagine the blizzard that hit me from the loose snow churned up by the propeller as the plane moved away.

First thing next morning I was still working at the computer when suddenly Max ran onto the lake barking. This behaviour was completely out of character. To my amazement, there came Nimpo Nick again—he'd snuck over the ridge and landed right between Big Island and the shore, and with the computer humming, I never heard him coming. (I usually tie the dogs up when I hear a plane, as they invariably chase it and the pilots are full of stories about dogs running into propellers.) Nick had zipped in early before work because he had lost an expensive pair of prescription glasses. When he had visited on the previous day, he had taken off his snowsuit in the cabin but forgotten it when he went back out to the plane to deal with the skis; once outside, however, the wind was nippy and he asked Mary to fetch the suit. The glasses had been in a pocket. Nick needs them for close work so did not notice that they were missing until after he had arrived home.

He was worried that they had fallen out when he was lying in the snow chipping the ice off the skis. But as I walked to meet him on the lake, I happened to see the glasses on the packed trail next to the waterhole. When Mary fetched the snowsuit, she had stepped off the trail into the soft snow alongside just there, and gone for a skate. The glasses must have fallen out of the pocket then. However, I had been walking back and forth on that trail, even pulling tobogganloads of boards up to the house, and would surely have either noticed the glasses or mashed them further into the snow. I think Max must have found them and played with them. He likes to chew spiky things like twigs or bits of wire sometimes. (He did a real number on the radiophone aerial when

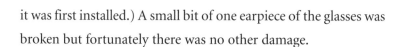

it was first installed.) A small bit of one earpiece of the glasses was broken but fortunately there was no other damage.

The best twenty-six boards have been stacked in my living room. They take up half the cabin. I can't get at my books very easily but it is the only place where the boards will stay completely dry. Fifty-four of lesser quality are now slung across the ceiling joists under Cabin Three's roof and the real scrap stuff, the twisted slabs and occasional wedge-shaped or badly split board, are all in a loose pile on the piece of waterfront nearest to the logging site, where they will stay until the ice goes out. Ten more boards were cut from a single straight, dead lodgepole across the lake. These were 5 cm thick and after I'd got them home, I laid them on the ice in front of the cabin and I ripped them into thirty-six two-by-fours. These will make the strapping for the porch roof. They are very strong and heavy, really straight-grained, but rather knotty.

Because it never quit snowing, the hauling never became easy. Even now, so late in the year, there are still 30 cm of loose snow on top of the lake with a layer of overflow underneath. If the wind is blowing, the snowshoe trail disappears within minutes and the only way to find it is by falling off it. So every day, and sometimes every hauling trip, I would have to break trail with the snowshoes to ensure that the toboggan stayed on track.

In case you are beginning to think I did a superhuman job, I have to confess that I had help with all this work. Three years ago some skiers were here and one of them wanted to come back and bring his girlfriend. He asked if they could work to earn their cabin fee, so what else could I give them to do?

Paul is an interesting person. He's a journalist and a photographer, but his main passion is history, particularly Canadian exploration. He has latched onto a lesser known explorer named George Back (I say "lesser known" for few people recognize his name now, but he had some repute in his day: Charles Darwin quoted Back's observations on permafrost in *The Voyage of the Beagle*). Back made four expeditions in the Canadian north, three of them along rivers, one of which now bears his name, and the fourth in the Arctic Ocean. Paul intends to follow the Back River next summer. He and a buddy will travel with canoes but will have to manhaul them across frozen lakes at the start of their journey. Dragging boards from the mill site to the cabin would be, we all conceded, excellent practice for this venture.

Paul and Liz struggled in conditions under which I would have abandoned the job long before. On one occasion, we had quite an interesting storm. During the morning a fine-flaked snow whirled upon a rather unpleasant wind from the northeast. It was never strong, but it was enough to bite our faces and keep filling the trail with snow. Suddenly, in mid-afternoon, the wind swung round and came from the south. We were on the lake at the time: Paul and Liz were each dragging loads and I was walking home with the ladder hung on my shoulder.

At this point it started to snow very thickly and it beat very hard against the sides of our faces. As we reached the cabin, the sky miraculously cleared and above us was a bright blue hole through which hot sun shone. It was dead calm—just like summer. All around, however, was a solid wall of smoky-looking snow cloud. Within a few minutes it started to snow and blow again, but this time the wind was a screaming gale from the opposite direction. The blue, warm spot had been the exact eye of the storm.

Liz Hauling Boards

The ten days that my visitors were here were the best of the winter. It actually got above freezing once or twice during the afternoon. This, however, was not all good because the fresh snow became very sticky and clogged on our skis. One day I took everyone to Octopus Lake. It was a fabulous morning and the views of Wilderness Mountain were

spectacular. I wanted to see if Chateau Bob was still standing after the big lean it developed last summer. Surprisingly it was still upright, although you could see very little of it; the snow flowed over it like a blanket and only a tiny triangle at one of the gable ends was visible.

9th Mar 99

Today is something of a celebration. There are two reasons: yesterday I finally finished going through the current draft of *Lonesome: Diary of a Wilderness Dog*. That was the book I was working on when you were here last spring. I will read it one more time before I print off a copy to present to a publisher, but whether or not I'll have time to do that before I leave for the spring book tour I don't know. It's not just the reading, which I can do in the dark as long as the batteries are full enough to run the computer, but the printer, which jams if more than one piece of paper is placed into the slot. I must sit beside it and feed each sheet individually. The printer is so slow that running off a full-length book takes two days! Fortunately the days are now very much longer—the sun rises in the middle of Louise O'Murphy's back (that's the group of three small peaks across the lake) and sets over Migma Mountain, which is next to Mount Monarch—so I should have enough sun. The printer takes quite a bit more power than the computer.

The other part of the celebration concerns the new cabin. Yesterday was the first time this year I was actually able to work on the structure. I prepared a work platform on the porch joists (having first dug them free of snow, of course), drilled holes for and pounded in bridge spikes to anchor the plate logs, measured distances, prepared the notches for the remaining six rafters and got two of them up. They frame the gable end and I will board that in before I raise the remaining four.

Although I have done no work on the building, I have thought about it a lot and I decided that I needed an extra cross-log to tie the plate logs together at the ends. I cut it from the meadow near the cabin. It was green and I wondered how I was going to haul it home. I snowshoed a trail back and forth a few times, making it as straight and firm as possible, but there were small ups and downs I could not avoid. At first I put the heavy end of the log on a toboggan and tried pulling it from the front. At the first bump, it stuck. The tail of the log dragged in the snow and I couldn't budge it. So then I got a rope and put it on the rear end of the log and pulled from there. This worked very well as the pulling raised the back of the log from the snow and the nose, on the toboggan, slid easily.

One night not too long ago, the northern lights were spectacular. I've seen them only a couple of other times through the winter and they were not very bright. But on this occasion a solid green glow sat in the northern quarter of the sky and brilliant dancing waves and curtains flowed and flickered overhead. A wonderful display of cold flames started over Halfway Mountain, then moved slowly to Louise O'Murphy, where it stayed but flickered for hours. It was as bright as full moonlight. I didn't bother to light the lamp when I got up but fired up the stove and cooked and ate breakfast by aurora-light.

It was dark and the moon and stars were shining when I started this letter. Now it is long after sunrise, but I cannot go outside yet for I have bread baking in the oven. When Paul and his friend flew out, the last of my supplies that were stockpiled at Nimpo came in on their pickup plane, and these included a number of firebricks, the kind used to line stoves. These were to be used as an experiment for building a stone oven. You will remember Uli Augustin's wonderful soapstone stove at Black Creek. I was so impressed with the flavour of the bread we baked in it that I have been inspired to try something along those lines here. I cannot quite see myself buying a stove like Uli's, though. Even by getting a "deal" because he installed it himself, the stove cost him $11,500. I thought I'd start a little more modestly by putting firebricks on the floor and partway up the walls inside the old barrel heater. (I would have lined the roof, too, but had no means of fastening the bricks up there.) I tried my firebrick oven a week ago with the loaves in bread pans, in case I had to transfer them to the old stovepipe oven in a hurry, and the result wasn't too bad. However, the heat in this makeshift oven is very uneven, being much greater at the chimney end and virtually non-existent by the door. The bread doesn't have that wonderful stone-oven taste either. Today I think the stove has become too cool. The cabin is certainly nippy and my feet are freezing under the computer desk. The firebricks don't seem to retain the heat very long. I guess the stove needs some sort of insulation on the outside. Maybe if I surround it with rocks to make a heat radiator, it would work better.

The bread is finished. I'm going to have a piece, hot and steamy, dripping with butter, and a final cup of tea, before taking myself onto the building site. It's going to be marvellous working in sunshine today. Yesterday was cold and grey with a mean little wind. I wore three sweaters and two pair of long johns but still I got cold feet, hands and ears.

I wonder if I am going to get the porch roof finished. There are only five weeks left before I have to be in Victoria to launch *Nuk Tessli: The Life of a Wilderness Dweller*, and I'll need to be at Nimpo at least a week before. Every time I get mail, it includes an exciting bunch of faxes from the publisher, sent to me via Mary. The marketing person is handling the final organization of the slide show tour. Thirty shows so far between Vancouver Island and Edmonton, with a small detour to Medicine Hat on the way. The thought of all that driving and having to walk the dogs on leads while they yank, yank, yank, in dreary little suburban areas makes me groan. Still, it is my trade-off. Without these tours, the books would not do nearly so well, and I would not be able to live in the bush for the rest of the year.

17th Mar 99

There has finally been a whole week where it did not snow. It was not always very good weather—often cold and grey and windy—

but I was able to make a lot of progress with the roof. Boards were put on both the porch gable end and the inner gable wall that will house the door into the attic. Plus I fitted a small, four-paned window in the gable end facing the mountains to give light to that part of the room. Once again, as I did in the fall, I find the pockets of my pants full of nails. A different size in each pocket. I always forget this until I undo the belt holding my pants up—to go to bed or the outhouse or whatever—and then my pants fall to the ground with a great crash!

However, the weather god decided I'd had it too good for too long. To make up for a snowless week, it dumped 35 cm in one night. All very pretty but another major digging out and shovelling needed everywhere. The clothesline got completely buried this time. The old loose snow on the lake had not settled and this extra stuff means it's now knee deep on the ice and the overflow is terrible. Last Sunday was a fabulous morning again and as Nimpo Nick had not been by for a while, and it was just the sort of weather that would tempt him to visit, I called out and warned him how bad the lake was. Sure enough, he had been planning on coming in.

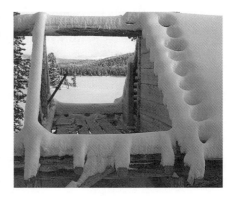

I have never seen so much loose snow so late in the year. One of the jobs I must do before I leave is take a canoe across the lake so that I will have a means of crossing the river if I hike home in June. I am going to have to snowshoe a trail over first, as I will never be able to drag a canoe in this. A couple of weeks ago I had to shovel off the roof of the canoe shed as there was such a huge pile of snow on it, it started leaning toward the lake. So now the canoes are walled in with mounds of massive lumps of rock-hard snow that I will have to chop away to get at the canoe. I'll have to strengthen the roof before next winter.

Since that snow dump I squeezed in two more productive days. Yesterday morning was absolutely fabulous: the first completely cloudless sunrise of the year and the mountains hard and bright and gleaming, new-snow-white against a blue, blue sky. But as with every break in the weather we've had this year, by evening a thick, white haze had crept over the sky from the west. And this morning it was snowing again—not a lot, perhaps 8 cm for the whole day, but even that amount, combined with a gusty wind, makes it impossible to work on the roof. I have now got all the rafters up and about three-quarters of the strapping. The strapping is taking a while because they are my own homemade two-by-fours and, as you know, cutting with the Alaskan Mill is not a hundred percent accurate: each one has to be adjusted for each rafter.

There are so many other jobs I could be doing—spinning the extra wool I still need for my sweater (so far I have sheep, bear, both dogs, highland cow, alpaca and mountain goat prepared), mending dog packs, sewing clothes, income tax (a two-day job, as the whole year's finances have to be sorted out), canning meat; but I cannot get myself organized to do anything when the roof is hanging over my head. And time is marching on. Just over two weeks before I have to leave.

While I have been writing, it has grown dark. The wind and snow have been getting worse and some furious gusts have been slamming into the cabin again. Up to this year it has been unusual to have wind from the south, but this winter the south winds seem never-ending. In March in some years I have sat on top of Avalanche Mountain in shirtsleeves. And I have sunbathed out on the ice. This year, apart from three partial afternoons when my visitors were here, and one other afternoon in early January, there have not been any days when the temperature climbed above freezing, even in the sunshine.

It's bread-baking day again tomorrow. I'm going to try a different arrangement of bricks in the barrel stove to see if I can improve the way it works.

19th Mar 99—sunrise

Minus 25°C again. There's been more cold weather this last month than for the whole winter. The water hole shrinks inward as well as freezing over the top during cold spells and it is rapidly getting very small. I can no longer dip a bucket in but must take a small pot to scoop the water out. I hope it lasts until I leave because cutting through the ice at this end of the year, when it is a great deal thicker than at the beginning of winter, would be a real chore.

Yesterday was dull and there was such a cold wind I had to work for part of the day in my down coat. I've never looked at myself in the mirror when I have ear-protectors on and the hood of my jacket pulled over them, but it must look very funny. The highest pieces of strapping were still to do and each one involved a lot of awkward wriggling and climbing up and down, all exacerbated by the bulkiness of the coat. At the end of the afternoon, a curious brilliant blue piece of sky appeared over the North Ridge. The cloud, which was otherwise unbroken, simply ended in a solid line. Gradually the edge moved south and suddenly the sun was shining and it turned into the most beautiful calm, golden evening. How wonderful it is going to be to have that sunshine coming into the new cabin. Every time we have a beautiful sunrise or sunset, I imagine looking at it from the luxury of a nice soft seat. Now, with the west windows of Cabin Two solidly walled in by snow, I have no afternoon sun or view up the lake at all from inside.

The calm, soft evening would have been perfect for raising the sheets of metal, but by the time I had finished the strapping, it was too late to start. However, I am now ready to go. All I need is the weather. There are eight pieces of metal to go up, plus two ridge caps. There is an extra strip of flashing to place at the top of the roof as well because I miscalculated on the length of the metal. Fortunately I had the flashing to hand. Even so, the overhang at the eaves is shorter than it should be, but as most rain or snow falls horizontally here, even a large overhang would not keep the walls dry. But the same wind that puts the water there dries it off just as quickly and it never sits on the walls for long.

The sky was clear all night but now a thick fog has obscured it, and the sun (which has appeared just to the left of Louise O'Murphy's bum; that shows the equinox is close) is simply a vague, yellowish blur. However, there is no wind or falling snow at the moment. I will have to wait an hour or so until it warms up a bit as my fingers will stick to the metal when it is this cold. The other day, when I put the first two ridge cap sections on, every time I reached into the bucket for screws, dozens of them stuck all over my fingers as if my hands were magnets.

It's Friday today and therefore possible that Nimpo Nick will attempt to come in this weekend. So I am getting all the mail ready to go and will print this off.

By the way, I knitted Betty a hat spun from Taya's fur with bands of bear and goat fur for a design. I will send it to her when

I mail her a copy of *Nuk Tessli: The Life of a Wilderness Dweller.* Your copy of the book will also be in the mail as soon as I get some from the publisher.

Love
Chris

"What a lovely way to spend my fiftieth birthday—
with Spotted Dick!"
—Lynda Tedesco, Nuk Tessli guest book, 1997

21st Mar 99

Dear Nick,

All of a sudden it was warm. Plus 10°C. Everything dripped; the brown metal roofing was hot to touch; I stripped off, on top of the roof, down to shirtsleeves; the wind was soft and warm like summer and very gentle for two whole days. And that is what it took me to finish the porch roof.

I was just about to drag the first piece of metal out of the cabin when Nimpo Nick and a friend arrived. Nick was in a visiting

The Roof is On !!!

mode, and he spent an hour fooling around with some electrical stuff for me—one was a device to stop my solar batteries from overcharging, which they do if I am not using the computer, and the other, believe it or not, was a rig for an electric light. Up to now I have always used kerosene lamps or candles for illumination, even when working on the computer. The keyboard is so situated that the light from the screen doesn't reach it properly but angling the kerosene lamp effectively was always a bit of a problem, as it got in the way of the mouse! Nimpo Nick supplied a 12-volt bulb that is connected, like the radiophone, directly to the two deep-cycle batteries; it does not, like the computer, have to be plugged into the inverter. The sun was shining brightly when he tried it to see if it worked so the full effect was not apparent until the evening.

Finally it grew dark and I switched the light on. It was so **bright**! I thought at first I was going to have to put sunglasses on to read. The cabin looked very strange with the unfamiliar illumination. The light is rather white and harsh and it is still fairly concentrated, so part of the cabin remains shadowy—also, I don't have a very long cord at present so it has a limited range. But what a difference! I can see what is happening to the food on the stove without needing to use the flashlight. And there is no stink of kerosene to put up with either. The kerosene lamp still has a valuable purpose, though. The only electric lamp I possess is a clip-on one I bought for a craft fair booth. Here, there is nothing suitable to clip it onto; it needs something that will elevate it high enough to spread light where I want it but heavy enough so that it will not tip over. Ergo, the good old hurricane lamp in its new mode.

It was midday already when Nimpo Nick and his friend left and I rushed out to the building and managed to get on six pieces of metal before the tree shadows from the mainland touched Big Island and it was time to quit. Sometimes the wind stopped completely and it felt distinctly odd to be at the building site without any sound of air movement whatsoever. I kept waiting for something to happen. The noise, as I bashed holes in the metal with a punch for the screws, was like the crash of cymbals made from garbage can lids. It echoed with sharp claps from across the lake. There were two more sheets of metal to go when I quit that day, but before I could place them, I first had to determine the exact length of the overhang, trim the two-by-fours, and prepare and attach the facings.

The facings were cut from a green log that I had already peeled and hauled from the swamp on the toboggan track I made earlier this month. I had just ripped the log in half when in came Nimpo Nick again, with Mary this time, for a last winter visit. Their plane noise must have disturbed an avalanche from Avalanche Lookout, for it tumbled down as they flew by.

Well, the visit with Nick and Mary was great, but all the time I was wondering if the miraculous windless weather was going to last.

Squaring off the gable end was time-consuming because of having to run up and down the roof grid for every little adjustment. As I did not have four hands, nailing on the facings necessitated all sorts of manipulations with string and hammers and nails while my legs were hooked into the roofing grid. And then fitting the last two pieces of metal was awkward as I had no roof grid left to stand on. However, because the snow was so high at that end of the building, I was able to wriggle ladders around and eventually reach everything without too much problem.

Then came the painful part: putting on the remaining extra flashing and the ridge caps. I could have done these jobs from the ladder, but it would have meant moving it every couple of minutes and it was far quicker to sit astride the ridge and hitch myself along. The whole of my weight was concentrated on the sharp V at the top of the ridge cap: each time I shuffled back to the ladder for another piece of metal, I could hardly walk. There was nowhere to set down tools and I had to stuff hammer, punch and screws about my person. I lost quite a few nails and screws as they skittered down the metal into the snow, and tried not to imagine myself skittering after them.

But it was done. It grew cloudy toward the end of the day. It was still possible to see a vague yellow disc where the sun was just hovering at the edge of the mountains when I put the last screws in along the eaves, but the air stayed dead calm. I was so exhausted, both physically and emotionally, I did not know whether to laugh or cry. I didn't even look at the building—I still needed wood and water for supper. Normally I would do these things before starting my daily carpentering, but I had not wanted to waste one minute of the calm.

I was just in time. On the following morning the clouds raced fast from the south and sure enough, not long after sunrise, the wind got up—not more than a stiff breeze, but it would have been too strong for me to handle the metal. I still need to work on the gable ends to block all the holes and gaps between the boards so that snow cannot blow in. As some of this is high ladder work it will be better done now while the snow gives me an extra boost. But with this wonderfully warm and otherwise very timely weather, another job is now more urgent—canning meat. Even the biggest lumps I had flown in at the beginning of winter are thawed right through. I cut up the first batch this morning and will can it when I light the fire for breakfast tomorrow (meat requires a roaring stove for a total of three hours or more so is best processed early). While it is hissing away I will cut the second batch and do the third and final lot the day after. That should give me about three cases of pints to add to the two cases I already have. Mary has two more big lumps stored in her freezer and I will process those in June; altogether that will last me through to next winter with quite a bit to spare. With luck I might not need to buy any at all next fall—or perhaps I'll get a ham or a lamb instead of my usual half beef. I love roast meat but can have it only in the winter, when the meat will keep without having to be preserved.

Mary and Nick took my last loaf of bread away, so I baked again this morning, as well. I have now constructed a pretty elaborate firebrick oven in the barrel stove. But there are so many bricks in there now that there is room for only one loaf at a time. It baked perfectly but even with the double thickness, the bricks cooled too quickly to do the second loaf and I am finishing that one off in the stovepipe oven. Now that the bottom of the stovepipe oven has burned out, it is almost impossible to control the temperature. I've already managed to blacken one end of the loaf although it is not yet cooked.

The only other jobs I will attempt today are digging out the canoe so I can take it across the lake, and shovelling off the new outhouse roof. The temporary roof of boards and tarps that we made last year has done good service but from the air that blue tarp shines like a beacon and it will be nice to get that eyesore out of the way. I have an extra piece of metal that I did not order (but paid for)—it will be perfect for the outhouse. Fitting it will be much easier to do now, when I can reach it by standing on the snow, so I want to finish it before I leave.

3rd April 99

The outhouse roof and the battens for the gable ends were slowly finished—soon the weather was back to snow showers and −25°C temps in the morning with no thaws during the day. At this time of year I get a great craving to see and smell bare ground again. Usually there are a few tiny patches of warming earth around the bases of sunny trees by the end of March, but there is no scrap of ground free of snow at this moment. During the hot spell while I was working on the roof, a sudden flush of migrant birds travelled through. There seems to be a mini east/west migration route over my lake, no doubt because of the gaps through the mountains to the coast. I saw four species on those two days, including a grey-crowned rosy finch: grey-headed race (how's that for an elaborate bird name) that until now I have observed only in the high alpine, in summer. None of the migrants stayed. Even the juncos (those sparrow-like birds with dark heads that pecked crumbs from the cabin porch when you were here) kept on going, and they are hardy little beasts. I guess they need the open ground to find food.

There are still 30 cm of snow on top of the ice on the lake. It is fairly well crusted and a plane will not sink into the overflow, but I still cannot walk on it without skis or snowshoes. Dragging the canoe across the lake was very hard work and I took it only as far as the little beach and not up to the trailhead. As long as I have it there, I won't have to cross the river if I hike home in the spring. (There's a story in the new book about how I tried to do that one year and got washed away.)

A couple of days ago there was a full moon, the fourth of the year. I measure the progress of the winter by the moons and always

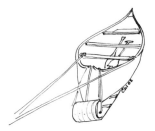

Hauling the canoe across the ice

look forward to the ethereal combination of pink, sunrise-painted mountains and setting moon. All the other full moon sunrises were cloudy this year and on the day of this full moon it was snowing. But it suddenly cleared the following evening and I went out onto the lake to watch it emerge through soft pink ribbons of cloud over Louise O'Murphy. The next morning was absolutely cloudless. I cannot see any of the western sky from this cabin right now because of the deep snow on that side, so tried to judge the timing of sunrise from the colour in the east and trudged out on snowshoes (in −25°C temps) to the viewpoint on Big Island. Just as I got there, the very first touch of pink coloured the top of Mount Monarch—and, at the same time, the last pinprick flash of moon disappeared behind Anvil Mountain.

The following morning (ah, how wonderful not to have to work on that damn roof!) I was out even earlier and skied to a point along the little ridge between my place and Avalanche Lake. The moon (with a slight fuzziness to its lower right quadrant) was perfectly positioned over Migma Mountain by the time the sun rose but there must have been fog or cloud on the Chilcotin, for there was very little colour on the peaks. There are some quite attractive views along the top of that ridge—I'll have to consider making a hiking trail along it.

Skiing was something I could now do a lot more of and I was determined to cover as much ground as possible in the time I had left. However, after years of cross-country skiing when I first came to Canada, and several winters with the heavy barn-board-like backcountry skis I now possess, I remain a terrible skier. Principally because in the tight, steep, forested areas, where there is no room to snowplow, I don't know how to stop. The backcountry skis are equipped with a set of skins. These are made from a synthetic material with a texture based on sealskin. Tough fibres attached to the bottom of the skis point backwards like hairs on a stiff-furred pelt. They are so efficient, one climbs mountains like a fly on the wall, and going up is therefore easy. Getting down, however (for me), is not. Most skiers remove the skins so they can swoosh down faster but even with them on I still find myself out of control. Down the worst bits I have even been known to shuffle backwards. But who cares how I get around, as long as I enjoy myself?

On the day of the full moon, it being such a brilliant, fabulous morning, I went up to Avalanche Lookout at the top of the

North Ridge, where I took you guys when you first arrived—almost exactly a year ago today if you can imagine. I do not possess a watch but it probably took me a good two hours to trudge to the treeline. In summer, most of the terrain above it would be rockslide and I would choose a route further east where a long, boggy meadow provided easier passage to the alpine. But now only the bigger boulders of the rockslide poked through the pillowy sweep of snow.

Above me there was the sharp calligraphy of some kind of activity on the snow and I plodded over to investigate. A squirrel-sized animal had emerged from a hole and run over the surface. Suddenly the marks became confused and the snow was churned and spattered with spots of bright blood. Framing the tracks were the twin prints of large beating wings. But the creature had escaped. Paw prints continued, erratic and lurching now, and the bird pounced again. But still the blood-spotted feet were able to run and the tracks disappeared through another hole by a rock. There were a few knee-high krummholz bushes about and squirrels will live wherever there is a cone to eat, but I think this animal must have been a pika. These pretty little creatures are about the size of guinea pigs and similarly tailless. They live in rockslides and do not hibernate but survive the winter by harvesting plants and drying them on sheltered, rocky ledges, then storing the hay in cavities beneath the boulders. They are common animals in the mountains but they dive into their labyrinthine world at the slightest hint of danger, so are rarely seen. As for the predator, it might have been an eagle, for they soar over the mountains when the winter thermals are right. Owls are rare up here but I occasionally hear their hooting when the birds migrate through in spring and fall.

During the winter, every time I broke trail up the mountain, it promptly dumped snow again and obliterated all my hard work. But now the snow had settled quite well and it was fairly easy going up. It was too warm to wear a coat until well above the treeline, but up top a tiny wind started and it was bitter, even with my feather jacket zipped tight around my ears. It was too cold to stop more than a few minutes, but I did the usual sweep of my "Queendom" (as Janis so delightfully described it in the guest book) through the binoculars. Many more mountains than those that could be seen from the cabins were now visible. They were clear but backed with grey cloud, from which remnants broke off and sailed raggedly into the cold blue sky. Mauve shadows trailed after them, undulating over the ridges and hollows of the land. The thread of my ski track looped down the wind-sculpted slopes to where it became lost in the trees. Far below was my lake, its blinding surface scored by plane tracks and the patter of activity around the cabins; the buildings themselves, however, were hidden. Behind was the sharp rise to the dark-forested plateau encompassing Octopus Lake where Max almost met his Waterloo on the frosty bridge. A whole slew of peaks lay beyond; dominating them was Wilderness Mountain—at 2,800 m the highest summit in the immediate area (but still a baby compared with the 4,000 m peaks to the west) and one of the very few with an official title. Peaking over its left shoulder, some 100 km distant, was the ethereal bulk of Mount Waddington, 300 m higher than Monarch and the highest mountain in the Coast Range.

Now for the tough part—coming down. The snow was far too wind-packed and glazed for my paltry skills. I tried taking the skis off but kept crashing through the surface, and it is too rugged and potholey up there to walk in those conditions. So back on with the skis and the usual elaborate zigzags with the occasional undignified backward shuffles. Some years, the rocks along the edge of the North Ridge blow clear and it is possible to climb to the summit with boots alone.

So it was something of a relief to reach the softer snow, but the sun had warmed it and it clogged monstrously to the skis. Apparently you can get stuff to spray on the skins to stop that. As long as I was moving fairly quickly it was fine, but the instant I stopped I would have to plod over to a patch of shadow and scrape all the gumbo off. I managed to have a wonderful long glide over the rockslide where I had seen the pika tracks but I dreaded the thought of the long descent through the forest. As soon as I hit the trees, however, the snow texture changed again. The surface had melted in the sun but it had gone past the sticky stage. However, it was pretty icy so I had some spectacular crashes. I wouldn't mind so much but now that my knees are shot it takes me forever to get back on my feet!

Love
Chris

"That mountain Louise O'Murphy reminds me of the awesome Spotted Tom? Harry? no, that's Dick."
—Rene Lemay, Nuk Tessli guest book, 1996

15th June 99

Dear Nick,

A cup of freshly ground decaf Sumatra and a piece of cake at my elbow—but they are not, I am afraid, being enjoyed on the deck as we did so often when you were here, for at present it is dumping rain: a good day, therefore, to catch up on computer work. I'm rewriting a book proposal. At Nimpo, when I passed through on my way home from the book tour, I received the second German rejection of *Cabin at Singing River*, a *Lonesome: Diary of a Wilderness Dog* rejection from Orca Book Publishers, and another publisher rejected the murder mystery that's been doing the rounds for two years now. Three rejections for three different books in three days: that's got to be some kind of record. *Lonesome* is probably the most marketable, so I am reshaping the query letter and sample chapters and trying again.

A great deal has happened since I flew out of Nuk Tessli on the 5th of April. I left behind thick, deep snow that had not yet settled (although it had sunk low enough behind the cabin to reveal my washing line), but at Nimpo Lake, spring was trying— still a foot of snow on the ground, but at least sixty red-winged blackbirds were making a tremendous racket in the tops of the aspen trees. They are a well-known harbinger of spring over much of Canada, but they like reedy swamps and I've only seen them three times at Nuk Tessli. Just goes to show how different my ecology is from that of the Chilcotin only 20 km away.

I started off on the book tour with a few days in hand, which was just as well. The previous fall, the clutch had been slipping on the truck. I had hopes of getting to Williams Lake on it, but about 50 km down the road, a little bit this side of Kleena Kleene, the clutch plate fell right out onto the road. While I had been driving, I had passed a vehicle every few minutes; once stopped, it must have been a good half hour before someone came by. Thus the start of my glorious tour ended up with me being ignominiously towed back to Anahim Lake by Sam Whitefish. The replacement clutch would have to come on the twice-a-week freight truck, which wasn't due for another couple of days. I figured there was enough spare time for it not to matter too much, but surprise surprise!—when it arrived, the part was the wrong size. Sam said the auto parts place had even billed me for the right one but put the wrong one in the box. It was the chainsaw debacle all over again. The next freight truck wasn't due for another four days. Fortunately Sam had a friend who was driving out from town much sooner, and when the part arrived, Sam started work at once. He's good that way: he'll work all kinds of hours if he has to. I remember once having a small job done on the truck—I forget what, but as usual I needed it done instantly and it was a Sunday morning. The truck was drivable so I took it down to the shop. It was winter and well below freezing so I huddled over the pot-bellied stove, which was roaring. The heat that blasted out was melting plastered gobs of snow off another truck that took up most of the space in the shop. This vehicle had just been towed in—some young guy had rolled it the night before. Sam told me not to touch it, as the cops were coming over to see it: there was apparently some liquor involved. Right as we spoke, the phone rang. It was the cops. They were on their way to Sam's shop but they'd locked their keys in their Suburban: could Sam come and break in and get them mobile again?

Three days after my first attempt at leaving, and $700 poorer, I was finally on my way. I camped the night along the Duffy Lake road, among bare trees but snowless ground not far from Lillooet, and arrived to new spring green at the Horseshoe Bay ferry terminal late morning. It was a beautiful, brilliant, calm, hot, sunny day, the first, everyone in the ferry lineup was saying, for many weeks. The constant dumps of snow I had been experiencing at home had translated in the Lower Mainland to a dreary litany of rain.

On the 14th of April, I met Orca's marketing person at 8:00 a.m. outside the office in Victoria. We started the day of publicity with two radio interviews, the second of which was on a phone-in show. One elderly lady spoke with a strong Ukrainian accent about her pioneering days in the Peace River area. She compared her achievements to mine, at length, and indicated most firmly that I had it pretty easy compared with her. She'd had only $12 a month to survive on and oh the things she had to do to make ends meet. The interviewer looked quite embarrassed but I agreed wholeheartedly with her claims. I am not a pioneer and I have all kinds of alternative ways of surviving at my fingertips if I want them. I also live a life of considerable luxury and ease.

At five, we were due at the CHEK-TV studios for the *Live at Five* news broadcast. I was not actually on until nearly 5:30, and we were able to watch the fascinating way that the anchorwoman and technicians put together their program of live and prere-corded items. They all slotted together so smoothly and with absolute split-second timing, and yet the whole process seemed completely casual. Finally, while an advertisement was being broadcast, I was ushered into the seat beside the anchorwoman and told I would be on for a grand total of two minutes. For all that, it was an excellent interview, with all the salient points addressed. And two minutes is actually quite a long time on the screen if it hits the right audience. *Live at Five* is a well-watched show throughout Vancouver Island, and a number of people came up to me during the subsequent slide shows and said they'd seen me.

I spoke at the museum at Campbell River, to the naturalists' group on Quadra Island, at the college in Nanaimo, a bookstore in Duncan and a couple of places in Victoria before travelling to the Lower Mainland and giving three more slide shows there, then moved to the Okanagan. No matter which way you leave Vancouver, big hills have to be climbed. Halfway up the Coquihalla Highway, I wondered if I was going to make it. Even with my foot to the floor, the truck could not travel at much more than walking pace. Confident that I could expect a nice lump of income from the new book (each of the previous two had produced a several thousand-dollar royalty check a few months later), I decided to trade in the truck for a new (old) one. By the time I left the Okanagan, I was driving a gleaming white Suburban, as old as my "old" truck but in much better shape—and with a great deal more room in it. I didn't have the money at hand to buy it outright at that point so had to take out a car loan from a bank. Because I have no regular income, I very rarely purchase anything this way: it's pretty scary. But with so much driving still to do, I felt I had no choice. I got a bit of a shock on filling the gas tank—the tab came to $100! But it travels a long way on a single tank.

In Alberta I spoke at Canmore, Banff, Medicine Hat, Drumheller, Camrose, Edson, Hinton, twice in Edmonton, and Calgary. While in Edmonton, I was interviewed by Arthur Black, one of Canada's best known CBC radio personalities. Unlike all the other interviews on the trip, this one would be broadcast Canada-wide. Arthur had wanted me to go to Vancouver for the interview but that I could not manage, so a taped talk, studio to studio from Edmonton, was arranged.

Arthur Black is a fast talker and my brain seemed to shift into overdrive. I was not nervous but I felt that I was thinking at high speed and also talking very quickly. But I was able to catch the broadcast the following Saturday, while I was driving, and I was amazed how relaxed—and even sensible—I sounded. Arthur Black is an excellent interviewer and he had obviously researched the book—unlike some interviewers, who haven't a clue. I did another CBC interview for a local Edmonton station and although the researcher, to whom I spoke at length on the phone beforehand, seemed excellent, the person on the air was completely out to lunch. She even referred to my new book as a novel.

I like to visit the prairies—I love the openness, the sky, and the rich, strange ecology of the coulees. But it is always a relief to see the earth begin to tilt, to hear the sound of water splashing over stones, and smell the scent of pines and the freshness of the mountain snows.

And so the long day-and-a-half drive to Williams Lake via the spectacular road that runs beside the Columbia Icefield north to Jasper, and then, through Prince George to Williams Lake. Leaves were newly out on the trees, and bears were everywhere along the roadside, eating the dandelions. New leaves all the way from Williams Lake to Kleena Kleene, but Nimpo Lake, on the 2nd of June, was as bare and grey as when I had left it. My lake was, according to pilots, still frozen although it went out on the 17th of May last year, and the weather was bitter cold and grey with showery precipitation falling as snow.

However, I am now finally at home. Much later than intended—all kinds of things got in the way, even at Nimpo—

but I am sitting at my computer looking out over the lake, which on the 15th of June, has been open just over a week. At the moment it is windy and whitecapped, and clouds scud across a broken sky while the stark white mountains still hang heavily with snow. The buds on the bushes are tight-packed fists with little tips of green; not even the pussy willows are flowering yet. But oh how wonderful it is to be home.

24th June 99

It always seems to take me a while to get organized after I have been away. All I want to do is laze about and read. There is the inevitable major cleanup to tackle: the chips in front of the woodshed; the dog hair and flotsam that accumulated under the snow in the porch; washing blankets; the shelves and walls to be scrubbed and so on. Then there was the canoe to fetch from across the lake (I didn't need it because I flew in) and the logs for the new cabin's wharf to rescue; they had floated away with the exceptionally high spring runoff. It is difficult to design wharfs here, as there is such a large difference between water levels from one season to the next.

While I was outside, I visited our friend Uli and his soapstone stove, and I've been inspired to build an outdoor rock oven. I managed to find a flat-sided slab for a base, which I

manoeuvred into a gap between two huge boulders near the new cabin's porch. The walls are merely rocks balanced on top of each other and cantilevered at the top until they meet. Earth was thrown over the whole thing. I haven't tried to bake in it yet. I'm debating whether or not it would be possible to build one inside the new cabin. Uli's is a very classy affair, designed primarily as a heater rather than a bake oven. You put a hot fire in it twice a day and the rest of the time it radiates a wonderfully comfortable heat. When the firebox is cool enough—Uli's has a thermometer in the door—you rake the ashes out and throw the bread right onto the hot stones. One time when I stayed with him I made a huge batch of bread—there was generally a pretty full house at that place—and there was too much dough for the stone oven. I split it and cooked half in the propane stove: the difference in flavour was unbelievable. I'll play with the outdoor oven for a while before I finally decide if I should try to put one inside the next cabin.

If I do decide to build an indoor one, I'm going to need a very solid foundation. When I first started to think about it, I figured it could be constructed directly onto the rocks below the joists, but such an enormous hole gapes where the stove would have to be, it would take forever to find and haul enough boulders to fill it. So I've made a very solid log base, laying hefty half-logs between the joists close enough to touch each other, and supporting them with even heftier horizontals and thick posts underneath.

Part of the house cleanup involved making and repairing all the cushion covers, which were in a very tatty state. So I spent a day with my wonderful "new" sewing machine. It is a hand-turned Singer that a friend of Betty Frank's secured for me. A list of patented dates is engraved upon a little silver plate near the needle, the latest one being 1898. When it arrived last summer I had no time to look at it right away. But a client came into my cabin shortly afterwards, noticed it on the floor in its case, and said (in a broad Scots accent), "That looks exactly like my mother's!" This lady herself was no longer young—in her late seventies, I believe. She was not happy until we had dragged out the machine and she had shown me how to thread it.

This lady was wonderfully energetic, a good hiker, and rapturous about the granite boulders over which she loved to scramble. She had apparently done a lot of climbing in her youth. But her fascination with the rock went further than that because her father had been a stonemason. Most of his commissions were gravestones, but after the 1914–18 war, he got contracts to make war memorials. One of these is in Edinburgh and apparently quite famous. The monument is typical of the times: a massive stone angel supports a fallen soldier. The model for the angel was my client's mother. She said she used to take her children along and say (you'll have to imagine the Scottish accent): "There's your grandmother." If I ever go to Edinburgh again I will have to look up the memorial—and imagine the angel owning the identical sewing machine to mine!

What a boon a machine like this must have been to the early settlers who would otherwise have to make every scrap of clothing by hand. When I finished the pillows I hauled out the dog packs. The dogs beat them up so much on the rocks I usually have to make several repairs in a season. I decided the older one was simply not worth bothering with any more. The patches' patches have patches. I wasn't sure if the sewing machine would handle that stiff vinyl material, but to my amazement, the only hand sewing I had to do was fastening on the straps. The whole pack took about three hours to make—normally it takes two long days to do one by hand and I have no skin left on the end of my middle finger where the butt of the needle digs in.

The weather during the first week I was home was very summery. Warm, even at night, and mostly hot and sunny during the day. The leaves and early flowers started to erupt dramatically, but then it turned bitter cold with endless heavy, grey winds (I had to wear two sweaters, a coat and long johns to work on the house site). The leaves have not moved from their half-out positions since the rain began. At least the pussy willows along the waterfront are finally out; the species that grows there has deep yellow blossoms that shine like old gold coins against the grey of the rain-pitted lake.

Two days were required just to clean the building debris from around the new cabin. Everything was buried in sawdust and discarded offcuts of wood from the winter's work—just as much as there had been when I cleaned it up last fall. Washtubs full of wood bits went to the woodshed for kindling; loads of sawdust were dumped into the stove and burnt. I found all sorts of treasures in the form of nails, roof screws, etc., dropped and lost when I was working in the snow. The sawdust had insulated the ground and some of it was still frozen. Under the porch there was a great lump of waist-high snow, which was now shaded by the roof extension and barely melting at all. I finally shovelled it into the sunshine to get rid of it. It almost seemed a waste of time to clean up the work site so much when it is going to get just as bad again, but it looked so depressing with garbage piled every-where. The amount of work still to do does not seem half so formidable now that the area is tidy.

And although very little has been accomplished, I must leave again for Nimpo in a few days. An alpine plant enthusiast, a gen-tleman from Victoria who has been to my place on five different occasions, was eighty years old this spring, so I thought I'd do something a little different with him this year. I'm going to meet him in Williams Lake and drive him to Bella Coola, and we'll do side trips to alpine areas across the Chilcotin. Ted is an excellent hiker and it should be a fun trip.

I don't know what sort of journey I'll have to the road. The snow has gone from the far shore of the lake and most of the hill-side above it, but several patches gleam through the trees—there are still big drifts around the meadow behind the cabin, and everywhere I look it lies thickly well below the treeline. With luck the cold weather will have kept the snow around Wilderness Lake from melting too much: when the water is high on that branch of the river, the bridge by Octopus Lake is flooded and impossi-ble to cross. Also I am wondering how Max will make out. When

I was at the coast I stayed with a friend who had no close neighbours and I was able to let Max off the chain. He went berserk, of course, and he tore around in the tangled cedar forest, then suddenly yelped. I could not see any injury or swelling but for the next two days he walked on three legs, holding a back leg high. Slowly, over several days, he stopped limping, although he seemed a little sore once or twice during the remaining weeks of the tour. As soon as he started running round at home, the lameness started up again. Swimming seems to be the worst; even after a few metres in the water, he gets so stiff he can hardly move. I've felt both legs and cannot find any great difference in their shape. I'm worried that it might be hip displacement and therefore incurable. I can't keep a dog that cannot pack to earn his keep. And because he won't come when called, can't be trusted with livestock and sometimes fights with other dogs (although he's never shown any animosity at all toward humans), he will be a difficult animal to give away. He seems happy enough otherwise, eats well and runs around on three legs quite easily when he is excited. It would be a great shame to have to destroy him, especially as he is now just starting his most useful years. He's even getting better at flying. He hates it as much as I do and still cries all the time we are in the air, but he has become resigned to his misery and it no longer takes two of us to force him into the aircraft.

As I write, there is a tremendous twittering going on around the big dead pine tree that props up one end of the woodpile you and Ellen built by the new cabin. When I first arrived home, I was greeted by great squawks and shrieks—a family of hairy woodpeckers was in residence in a hole about three-quarters of the way up the tree. The babies must have been very small at that time, for I heard only faint but constant peeping. They grew rapidly and soon shrieked continuously for food, sticking their heads and then most of their bodies way out of the hole. They must have a very safe nest to make so much racket without danger from squirrels. Finally, yesterday morning, there was silence: the birds had flown. And today, three or four tree swallows are fighting like mad over the hole. A brand-new apartment complete with food supply in the form of discarded fleas and lice!

It quit raining for a short while and the sun gave a few watery gleams, but it is coming down hard again now and the swallows are flying so low they are almost touching the lake. Heavy, low clouds roll in from the east. There is not much wind and I took advantage of the calm this morning to bring the fuel drums round from the meadow where the biologist's helicopter left them. All four had some fuel in them—I decanted about five gallons into a can. Apparently, helicopter jet fuel cannot be used in a chainsaw but is close to kerosene and might be okay for the lamps. I'll have to try it sometime in the middle of the lake in winter, so if it flares up it won't burn the place down. The drums now lie ugly and yellow below the deck, waiting to be made into a float. I cannot leave them on the wharf: the water is so high right now, everything washes off it. When I walked on it a week ago, the wharf sank with my weight until the water almost reached the tops of my gumboots.

I can't build the float until some heavy spikes arrive. I have been expecting a planeload of supplies for the last couple of weeks. Cameron Linde (from the sawmill near Williams Lake) was supposed to bring a load of lumber and insulation to Nimpo Lake quite a while ago. He was going to fly in with his daughter and stay the night and then I would get a Beaver to pick him up and bring some of the materials. But when I called the float plane company they said there has been no sign of him so far.

Well, rain or no rain, I'm sick of being inside and I'm going for a hike. I haven't had time to go above Otter Lake yet. Not too long ago, Otter Creek was roaring so much that even with gumboots on, I had real difficulty in keeping my feet dry. I had to force my way far into the bush to get around the overflowing water. I was pleased to see that the footlog bridge I made last summer was still 30 cm above the water level. I have seen the creek even higher—one year a huge amount of snow melted all at once—but I think that this bridge will be safe. The other little bridge near the mouth of the creek has been washed against the fallen tree below it again. I'm always having to haul it back after the creek floods. I'll have to think of something better for that location.

And now it's the 27th of June and I must pack the computer upstairs and out of reach of any stray bears so that I can leave for my plant trip with Ted first thing in the morning. Chill wind, fog, drizzle and a few flakes of snow at present.

Cameron Linde arrived in a Beaver three days ago with his daughter and a load of freight, and another Beaver came yesterday to pick him up, this one carrying some of the one-by-three tongue-and-groove cottonwood and batts of fibreglass insulation. You wouldn't believe how fiddly it was to stack that tongue-and-groove into the plane. In the lumberyard it was banded in a sling and Cameron used that ancient homemade monster of a forklift he has in his yard to put it on his truck. But each piece had to be loaded individually into the Beaver. As soon as the bands came off the sling, the timber sprang into all kinds of humps and banana shapes and it was like trying to stack spaghetti. The seats were taken out and the door near the tail opened so that the lumber could be slotted in that way. I had no idea what a lot of work it was going to be to handle it. The pilot had squeezed in every last piece that he could; it must have taken quite a while to pile it in there.

Cameron had picked up the plywood and the insulation for me in Williams Lake, which saved me a lot of extra truck-freighting costs. But Floyd, the pilot who flies in here most of the time (he had brought the first plane in), says there will be at least eight Beaver loads altogether. To charter a Beaver costs $300. I hope I can defray some of the expense by having stuff come in on people's pickup planes.

When Cameron was shown the outdoor bread oven, he told me about some that he saw when he was visiting his father's family in South Dakota. It was not far from the place in the Black Hills where Custer made his Last Stand. Apparently the American army was camped there for a long time and they built a number of rock bread ovens to bake for the troops. The bakers even scratched their names on the rocks. Unfortunately, souvenir hunters have since taken most of the stones away.

I'm going to sign off for now so I can finish packing for the trip. I'll mail this when I reach the post office at Williams Lake in three days' time—truck willing!

Love
Chris

"Spotted Richard?"

—"Mean" Jack Rollo, note on a box of supplies, 1998

7th August 99

Dear Nick,

The first excitement on the grand cross-Chilcotin plant tour happened about halfway into Williams Lake. (No, it wasn't the truck breaking down this time!) The weather was warm, turbulent and excessively humid. It wasn't actually raining at that moment, but massive thundery-looking clouds were piled over the Chilcotin. Up in the sky I caught a movement and stopped the truck to look. Twenty-two enormous birds were riding a thermal, gliding round and round without a single quiver to their wide, board-like wings. My first thought was that they were sandhill cranes. I have very occasionally seen their tracks or heard them out on the Chilcotin and they are quite common east of Williams Lake. But I've never seen cranes riding a thermal before, and in any case these birds didn't look right. Their necks were not extended like those of cranes but tucked back like herons'. Through the binoculars I could see their beaks. They were pelicans. I knew that white pelicans nested further east on the Chilcotin and were present on Anahim Lake throughout the summer, but I had never seen them before, as they don't visit or fly over Nuk Tessli. I have also observed different species of pelicans in the tropics, but they usually sat on pilings or flapped cumbersomely close to the sea. I had no idea they were such fantastic soarers. When I checked in my bird book it was to find that their favoured travel technique is to ride thermals, sometimes so high that they are out of human sight, then glide to their feeding grounds. They may travel 110 km in a day this way.

Ted and I had a wonderful trip despite being dogged by an absolute deluge of rain for the first half of it. After making several small excursions we finally arrived at Potato Mountain, the crux of our expedition. Potato Mountain sits between Chilko and Tatlayoko lakes like a great lump of bread dough, having a broad, flat top right at treeline level. It is sandstone and therefore geologically very different from the volcanic interior of BC or the granite coastal mountains; consequently the flora are also very different. I had been up the horse trail at the north end before and marvelled at the flowers then; but I had no idea until this trip that the southern end of the mountain had a totally new range of species. On top of which, the day we climbed up there was finally sunny and we had a most glorious hike through a bonanza of flowers of every colour. As we travelled up the mountain, we passed through several different ecological areas. Lower plants that were in full bloom shrunk into the ground as we climbed, until they were either tight in bud or non-existent; by then other plants were dominant, until they too shrank into buds. It was a walk back in time. Most of the long, flat top was covered in snow but in the melted areas were a riot of blossoms, the predominant being a small flower called spring beauty, which is also known as the Indian potato. It's not a potato at all but has a thumbnail-sized corm as a storage organ for starch at the tip of its root, and the Carrier and Chilcotin Indians used to come up here in the spring and have great horse races and parties while they gathered them. The small white starry blossoms were so thick on the ground that they emulated the snowdrifts among which they grew. And all the time the sun shone, the creeks sang, and the surrounding mountains in their whipped-cream spring snow were glorious.

Potato Mountain has another claim to fame—fossils. On a previous trip I visited one of the main fossil areas near the top at the north end. The rock was composed of a solid mass of thumb-joint-sized shells, a very ancient species on which the ridges on the back run from side to side instead of radiating from the pointed end like those on modern shells. That fossil bluff overlooks a steep descent to Tatlayoko Lake. It was a wild, windy day when I was up there. I walked along a shelf

INDIAN POTATO
(Claytonia lanceolata)

141

with the bluff curving above me like a wave where the ancient sea had carved away its base. The shelf was littered with loosened shells that crunched under my boots. The wind roaring in my ears sounded like waves crashing and lapping at my feet, and as long as I looked toward the bluff, I felt as though I was walking along a beach. But when I looked the other way, there was nothing but a screaming drop of 1,300 m to the lake. It was quite disorienting to have the illusion of a seashore perched at pelican height above the ground. (Perhaps the pelicans weren't so misplaced after all!) In another area I found plant fossils: some kind of fern, I believe. On this trip Ted and I ran across a smaller bluff, which contained a few shells but also revealed some curious pieces of pencil-thick rod that the owners of the lodge, at which we stayed, told us were the tunnels left by a rock-boring clam. Pack dogs are great animals to have along when you are fossil hunting. They don't protest when you stuff a few extra rocks in their bags.

From Tatlayoko, we drove to Nimpo Lake and stayed a night at Mary's resort, then went down The Hill to Bella Coola. Inside the Tweedsmuir Park boundary, just before the top of The Hill, we passed two cyclists heavily loaded with gear. (It's a tough road for a bicycle, but you see a few occasionally.) Round the next bend we met a pickup truck, and shortly afterwards encountered a beautiful sow grizzly with three grown cubs bigger than she was. They would all have been three-year-old males. All four bears still had full winter coats with reddish gold tips that gleamed in the sunshine. There had been several reported sightings of these bears but I did not think we would be lucky enough to see them.

As we watched (sitting in the vehicle), the pickup we had just seen drove up behind us. In the back were the two cyclists and their bikes. The pickup driver had thought it best to take the cyclists past the bears to avoid trouble, which was very thoughtful of him; I must confess it never occurred to me to warn them. The bear family was below the road and already moving off into the forest. They were very relaxed and obviously completely unfazed by the vehicles, but I don't know how they would have reacted to a bicycle.

And then, at the bottom of The Hill (I won't bore you with the plants on the way—it took us the whole day to drive from Nimpo to Stuie!), just at the very last hairpin bend, we encountered a black bear with three tiny little babies all lollopy-limbed and teddy bear-headed, who entertained us for quite a while tumbling about and turning over stones to look for ants, just like Mum.

At Stuie we visited with Ron Mayo, the man we met last spawning season who is so knowledgeable about the bears. Ron is interested in every aspect of nature as well as the bears. The buildings at Stuie are half-drowned by massive cedars and firs: if the forest was left untended, a dense snaggle of hemlocks would grow up and smother the forest-floor plants. By judicious pruning, Ron has knocked back the hemlocks and encouraged a wonderful display of ground flora: bunchberries, princes pine and several species of orchid, most of which were in their prime. What a contrast to the lodge next door, whose property has been logged, plowed and turned into a putting green.

While we were poking happily around in Ron's yard, we heard a shot from the lodge's campground. People are always blasting off at bears—usually without any harm, although I heard of one guy who was so scared he fired at the bear right through his camper. He made two great holes in the camper but it was not known whether he had hit the bear: the park ranger went round at the time warning everyone that there might possibly be a wounded bear in the vicinity, but fortunately there was no other trouble. In this case, however, a bear had been killed outright. The victim was none other than Maple's cub, the young male bear that pursued us when we hiked to the confluence last fall. The young bear was old enough to leave his mum and it is usually at that age that they are the most nuisance. So far this young male had not done any damage, but he'd caused a number of frights and I guess it was inevitable that he would meet someone with an itchy trigger finger sooner or later.

On our last day together Ted and I tried to drive up one of the logging roads near Bella Coola. The pass was only 1,200 m in elevation but was blocked a long way below the top by tons and tons of snow. It had been gone from my lake, which is 400 m higher, for a month. But those mountainsides face the coast and receive the brunt of the precipitation coming off the Pacific. A number of glaciers tumble well below the treeline in that area, so snowfall is generally heavy, but the snowfall everywhere in the Pacific Northwest broke all records last year.

Renting one of Mary's cabins at Nimpo Lake, when I got back there after the trip with Ted, was a young woman called Sandra who was working in the area for a while. She was due to have a four-day weekend off and a hiking friend was visiting her, so I invited them to backpack home with me.

The friend, Lino, turned out to be quite a surprise. He was my age, an Italian immigrant who has been in Canada thirty years, but who speaks very little English and cannot read or write it at all. He came over here as a young man and worked for an Italian construction company digging ditches by hand and doing other labouring jobs for very low wages. He was raised in a village in the Dolomites, and obviously had very little formal schooling. In Vancouver he never strayed from his small immigrant group, so for most of his life he had little idea that there was any kind of existence other than the one he was experiencing. Three years ago he had heart trouble and was advised to take some exercise, so he started walking. He discovered that he absolutely loved to hike and began clocking up tremendous distances in a day. Sandra met him while tramping round the mountains near Vancouver and now they do a lot of walking together. Lino had never been backpacking before, or gone off a well-used trail, so the hike into my place was a big adventure for him. There was still a lot of snow in the high country but we had excellent weather and a great trip; we camped overnight by the creek crossing near Fish Lake.

I told them I expected a day's work from them (I was giving them a free flight out on a freight plane) and asked Lino if he could use a chainsaw. "Oh, sure!" he said confidently. "That's how I got this." And he pointed to a great scar on his face that went from his eye to his chin. He'd been cutting firewood at home and the saw had kicked back. And he hadn't used a saw a great deal since, so I thought it best that I do the limbing and bucking.

I put them to work at the site where I had cut all the lumber in the winter. There was a considerable number of tree parts—

stumps and tops—that were not suitable for building purposes, but that would make perfectly good firewood. The loop trail to Otter Lake goes through the site, and with all the debris and thick piles of sawdust from the lumber making, it looked a terrible mess. I sliced off the stumps and bucked up the other parts, and got my two helpers to split the wood and stack it under a big sub-alpine fir where a large snow-well always forms. The wood will be easy to find and dig out in the winter at that spot. Lino could use an axe with great facility. He said his father had made wood-en buckets and he used to split the pieces for it when he was a boy. But he had not done this work for forty years; he enjoyed himself so much I think he almost preferred the axework to the hiking part of the trip. If they had time, they were to scatter the thick wadges of sawdust so they would not be such a terrible eye-sore, and clean up the discarded brush that could be seen from the trail. The bugs were terrible and I did not expect them to finish that part of the job, but at the end of the day you could hardly tell that I had logged there; in a year or two when the sawdust crumbs have greyed, there will be virtually no sign of any tree butchering at all.

The year was advancing with frightening rapidity, but before I could get on with the cabin there were still other jobs that had to be dealt with. The most important of these was constructing the float. When I first came here, I built a wharf that jutted out into the water, but the Land Office wanted to charge me a whole separate lease for the privilege, and the insurance company wanted to class it as an airport and charge an exorbitant fee, so I cut the wharf back to the shoreline. This has made it difficult for the bigger planes to get alongside, as their wings fall foul of a beautiful, lichen-encrusted snag I do not wish to cut down. A float, being a non-permanent structure, would get around some of the regulations.

Most floats are constructed so that the drums are hidden under the dock area. The biggest wear and tear on drums is when the ice is going out. Some resorts drag their floats right out of the water for the winter but I did not have the resources to do that (i.e., a road and a pickup truck), and there was no way I was going to be able to push the drums underneath the float once it was in the water. So I figured out a design in which I could tie the barrels in at the ends after the float was in the water, and remove them again before winter. This would also make it easy to replace the drums when they wore out.

It took two days to round up all the logs and braces I would need and paddle them home by canoe. I built the frame on the existing wharf, then peaveyed it centimetre by centimetre toward the water. When it was almost ready to slide in, it would not go forward but simply rocked back and forth every time I put the peavey under it. But at last I managed to nudge it that final centimetre, and with a great *swoosh!*, it was launched. (And yes, I did remember to tie a rope to it and fasten the rope to a tree before it went in!) To keep the weight down I had placed only a few boards on the frame, just enough to give me something to stand on once it was in the water. I was surprised to find that the boards did not sink below the surface even when my weight was added, but I knew the logs would not remain buoyant for long without the extra support of the drums. I fitted the barrels into the spaces I had built for them on either end and tied two ropes over each barrel, cinching down first one rope and then the other until I had the drums more than half-submerged. I did this from the water with my knees jammed in the pointed prow of a canoe. The float has to be tied fairly loosely to the stationary wharf, as it has to be able to drop with the water level. The bright yellow barrels stand out like a neon sign, which is rather a shame as all my other building efforts have been toward blending the structures with the landscape. But the pilots will be much happier now when they bring in their planes.

The very next day, Nimpo Nick and Mary flew in. Proudly I stood at the edge of my new float ready to catch the Supercub's wing. Nimpo Nick stepped onto the float and *splooosh!* it lurched down and water rushed over both our feet! I am no lightweight and Nick certainly isn't; obviously two heavy people on one corner is not a good idea. But as long as I remember to counterbalance the float when someone steps on the other side, it works very well.

The Float

The next job was to fix the canoes. After all the firewood and lumber hauling I have done, the gunwales on both were completely shot and a lot of the fibreglass was cracking round the rim. There is no way I could make gunwales; no local material is long and straight enough, or pliant enough, to coerce into shape. So when I was in Williams Lake I bought thin plywood, then cut it into strips, and have now bolted it to both sides of the boats, inside and out. The strips imperfectly follow the curve of the boats so look scrappy and ugly, but they have made the canoes much stronger.

Then I had to do some fibreglassing, a job that I hate because it stinks and I get gobbed all over with the stuff and I never get the mix right. I don't know what went wrong with the first batch but it never set at all. Perhaps the hardener was too old. So I had to redo it a day later, but I'm still running into sticky areas I neglected to cover.

The first batch of bread I made after I got home was with the stovepipe oven, as I wanted to feed Sandra and her Italian friend in a hurry and could not afford to experiment. So it was a few days after I'd been back that I tried the stone oven for the first time. I lit the fire with brush and, after it died down a little, stuffed the oven full of split wood. When that was reduced to coals, I raked out the ashes, then tested the temperature by tossing in handfuls of flour. When it no longer scorched right away, I deemed it ready for the dough. But that first batch of bread did not cook properly and I finished it off in the stovepipe oven. The second time I tried it, I split the wood smaller and stuffed the oven full twice instead of once. And the bread was absolutely perfect. Every batch I've made since (about six to date) has turned out fantastic. The flavour is out of this world. I've discovered that it is not so much the fierceness of the fire that is important as the length of time it is burning. Three or four hours is about right. If I start it off at the same time as I begin the bread, the dough and the oven are ready at the same time. I've baked cakes in the oven, and also roasted potatoes for dinner. Tomorrow will be a real test as I will make three batches of bread. I'm expecting two separate groups of tourists on the day after. The stone oven holds two loaves slightly bigger than the ones I could make in the stovepipe oven, which makes each one about twice as big as a bread pan loaf. I will try and cook the first two batches one right after the other, but will probably have to put another fire in there to cook the last load. I don't mind baking late in the day in that oven, as it does not heat up the cabin. And I don't have to sit over the loaves and check them every two minutes like I did with the burnt-out stovepipe oven: now I simply toss the bread inside and forget about it until it smells done. The loaves taste best, of course, when they are baked directly on the stones, but I'll have to make one in the famous bear-tooth pan: I can't have a bunch of visitors without telling them the famous story of the bear break-in, how he chewed the pan, and how all the loaves of bread baked in it are consequently indented with the bear's tooth mark.*

So what with one thing and another, it wasn't until the 19th of July that I could finally do some work on the cabin. The first big job I tackled was framing the windows. I used the best boards from the stack of lumber that has been doing duty as a table in Cabin Two since last February. The joinery on the framing is by no means perfect but it is the best carpentry work I have ever done and I'm very proud of it. How sensuous is the surface of newly planed and sanded wood! I'm going to double-glaze these windows. Most of the panes will be fixed, but I want three of them to open and these need accurate wooden frames around the glass. My carpentry is not good enough for that, so I'm going to ask Uli to make them for me. He's a fine carpenter and will do an excellent job.

I couldn't work right through on the windows because not long after I got started, my architect friend, Alan Bell, and his family arrived from Vancouver. Alan leads a high-pressure life, often whizzing to places like Kuwait and China to discuss proposals for city complexes. To relax, he likes nothing better than to play with rocks, and over the years he has constructed all the

*See *Nuk Tessli: The Life of a Wilderness Dweller.*

stone steps and pathways around my cabins. Having had so much success with the outdoor oven, I was by this time completely sold on the idea of an indoor one. With an expert rock builder on the doorstep, I naturally put him straight to work. It turned out to be a much bigger job than I had expected. Alan manhandled huge rocks and cemented them into a structure that we referred to, as it progressed, as a gravestone, a sacrificial altar, a throne, an edifice and a mausoleum. That should give you a pretty good idea of what it looks like!

For the bottom of the oven, we chiselled off part of the huge rock beside the porch. There was a natural split to make a slab about a metre long, half a metre wide, and 15 cm thick. Elizabeth, Alan's wife, had read that wooden wedges are used for splitting rock and they worked far better than the metal wedges you and I used that first spring, when we broke up that huge boulder that was in the way of the foundations. Unfortunately Alan's slab did not travel to the stove site without breaking into a number of pieces, but cemented together, it still makes a more or less flat bottom to the oven. We worked incredibly hard for four of the five days that the Bells were here (we allowed one day for hiking) and got the structure's walls about three-quarters finished.

When I was in Vancouver last spring, I picked up an old furnace door for $20. It is inscribed: ENTERPRISE Foundry Co Ltd, Pt 1922, Sackville NB. My other stove doors come from Winnipeg and Vancouver, so I'm getting quite a Canada-wide selection of cast iron on the place. A welder at Anahim made me two flat straps with a hole in one end and we cemented these into the structure to hold the furnace door's hinge pins. The frame was built with firebricks in order to give the door something flat to shut against, but as the door hole was two brick lengths wide, I had to find something that would form a lintel. I never throw anything away; metal pieces have long resided in the crawl space of Cabin Two, and when I rummaged around down there with a flashlight, I unearthed an old chainsaw bar that had been worn out through lumber making: as a chainsaw part it was junk; as a lintel it was ideal.

Alan, Elizabeth, their son Andrew and a friend were to leave early in the morning and I switched on the radiophone so that I could hear when their plane took off from Nimpo. But instead of the float plane company's messages, I heard a call for an air ambulance from a place called Corkscrew Creek. I knew the name but I could not remember where it was. The patient, a woman, had been horseback riding and aggravated an old back injury. She was in a lot of pain and one leg had gone numb. She would have to be helicoptered out. When Floyd came in to pick up my friends, he told me that the patient was Mary. She had been on her annual horseback trip to see the flowers in the Itcha-Ilgachuz park, another volcanic complex north of Nimpo. I kept the radio on for a while and heard that the helicopter was having a hard time finding the horse camp. The pilot kept asking them to make smoke; they must have been hidden within the trees. Later I heard Nimpo Nick calling the chopper pilot and learned that Mary was being taken to Bella Coola. She is back home and recovering now but must be feeling very frustrated. She was laid low with this back problem once before and had considerable pain.

The day after my stove-building friends left, a couple of clients arrived—at last I could earn a little money. The visitors wanted to hike above the treeline; it was the first time this year that I have been to the North Ridge. Because the snow lay very late, the tiny plants that grow right on top of the ridges were still

Visitors and Max above my lake.

in full bloom. They are usually dried right up by now, so it was an added pleasure to see them.

Four days later, at the beginning of August, I was up there again with another couple. I wasn't expecting this party and when they got off the plane I said, "This is a surprise, who are you?" They said nothing—they just looked uncomfortable. And Floyd, the pilot, who is naturally taciturn, didn't enlighten me. Packs started to come out of the plane so I thought to myself, "Well, I guess they're planning to stay." I spoke to them a second time and still received no reply. And then it dawned on me who they must be. Last winter, a Swiss fellow who works for a log-building company at Anahim had told me he was getting married at the beginning of August and might send his parents in to visit me. I'd not heard a word from anyone since and so I forgot about them. "Sind Sie," I stumbled, trying to dredge up my rusty German, "die Eltern von Martin?" Upon which there were big smiles all round. They were excellent hikers and—a big bonus for me—very knowledgeable about alpine plants. Most of our conversation was not in German but in botanical Latin. All I would have to say was "Das ist ein *Campanula* (or *Senecio* or *Solidago*, or whatever) and we got on famously. They brought me a wonderful Swiss plant book that has absolutely everything in it, both lowland and highland—3,000 species and 4,000 photos. According to the distribution maps some are very rare; others are plants that have been grown in gardens and then gone wild—including things like radishes and marijuana! It makes North American field guides look puny.

Even though Martin's parents needed only the little plane to fly them out, I asked for a Beaver and paid the difference, which saved me quite a bit on yet another load of freight. Storage of lumber is becoming a big problem. Now the mausoleum is squatting in the middle of the cabin, there is very little floor space left downstairs. Two-by-fours and one-by-tens are piled on and around Janis's floorboards, and the attic porch is stuffed with the spaghetti tongue-and-groove.

I originally entertained the idea that I might be moving into the new cabin by Christmas but I can't see that happening now: soon I must abandon the building project yet again. In a couple of days I leave for the coast to speak at the 17th annual Sunshine Coast Festival of the Written Arts in Sechelt. I've never been to a writers' festival before, let alone spoken at one, and I would normally be very reluctant to be away in the summer, particularly as I've already had one trip outside this year. But this is a fairly prestigious engagement that will give me excellent publicity for the new book. The festival lasts for four days, and I will need two days at one end and three at the other for driving and shopping, so I will be gone for over a week. I could fly door to door—Sechelt's on the ocean and the festival committee is paying the tab—but the cost would be horrendous. And if I did that, I would not be able to swing by Williams Lake to pick up more building supplies on the way home.

Hisako arrived a couple of days ago to house- and dog-sit again while I am away. Poor Hisako, she has got lumbered again. When I asked her to look after the place this time I did not realize she would have two different groups renting the cabin plus a whole bus tour all to herself. I had planned to start hiking to the road on the 9th of August, but another bus tour sneaked in for that day. This one is a bit different from the usual groups, who are mostly retired Canadians from Victoria or the Okanagan.

The tour is run by the American Sierra Club. There are only fourteen of them (instead of forty) and they will be split into two parties and not three. The last one is supposed to leave around 2:30 in the afternoon, so at first I figured I could still start hiking on the 9th, arrive at Nimpo by early afternoon on the 10th, pack the truck, start driving early the 11th and be in Sechelt in good time on the 12th. But then Dave Neads, our local environmental activist, sprung an urgent request on me. He wanted to bring in a group of people who might be involved with the preservation of the Charlotte Alplands. They wish to be taken on a hike to the lookout. Among the crowd will be someone doing an article for the *Vancouver Sun* and *Beautiful BC* magazine. They want to come at lunchtime and stay until 7:30 p.m. I've asked Hisako to guide the second Sierra Club party so I can be here when the other visitors arrive. It is going to be a pretty hectic day.

Love
Chris

"When I go to London I always go to a special restaurant in the Strand that sells it. You only get a very small helping and it costs a lot of money."
—Ron Lunn, conversation, 1997

22nd Aug 99

Dear Nick,

The sound of an axe, driven by a powerful arm, smacks into a round of wood. The arm belongs to an Australian I "picked up" at Emily's in Williams Lake on my way home from Sechelt. You know how Emily's house is always full of travellers, especially now that her daughters are in university. The Australian is called Matt. He's about your age and a pleasant individual, but has not got your commitment to the wilderness. He'd rather hang out in places like India and Nepal (which is where he met one of Emily's daughters). He's a great scribbler and writes copiously in his journals, so I suspect professional writing will be a part of his life at some stage. He has also studied photography so is creative in a number of fields. He wears several earrings around the rim of one ear and has a small turtle tattooed between his shoulder blades. Although he's not had much experience with tools, he's worked very hard here and has packed and canoed home the scattered firewood on the site where we cut the building logs. He has a work permit for Canada and has been tree planting and brushing and is going mushroom picking in the Queen Charlotte Islands later on. Thanks to you guys I have so much firewood on hand that I didn't really need the stuff he brought home; however, it never hurts to have that kind of work done when testosteronic muscle is available. Once he has finished that, I'm going to have him start putting the tongue-and-groove on the ceiling. It will mean all the lumber up in the attic will need reorganizing. How difficult it is to build when you have no independent storage space—or can't just pop down to the store when you need the necessary pieces.

The Festival of the Written Arts at Sechelt was absolutely fantastic. A bookstore handles all the sales so all I receive is royalties (if I sell the books myself, I get the bookstore's 40%), and the royalties won't filter through for another ten months. However, I sold literally hundreds of books. I had a fabulous audience—the hall of 500 seats was jammed and they roared with laughter throughout the show. My slide show was scheduled for the Sunday afternoon, almost at the end of the festival, but the organizers had asked me to be there for the full four days, which I was delighted to do: they let me set up an art booth near the bookstore, and they even supplied volunteers to sit at it, so I could attend all the lectures. I've met only three other writers in my life before—it is always very morale-boosting to meet artists who have similar struggles.

Sechelt is on the mainland, but can be reached only by ferry from Horseshoe Bay just north of Vancouver. I spent the night in the truck on the Duffy Lake Road again and arrived at the festival buildings mid-morning. I was given a section of a hall to set up my wares—the space included a piano, which made a great display cabinet. While I was in the throes of arranging and pricing, I was introduced to a slim, tall man who had just arrived from Vancouver by float plane. As always when I meet someone, the name flew out of my head as soon as I heard it. He said something polite about my writing and I had to confess I had not heard of him. He gave me a funny look, then asked if I knew of a decent lunch place in town. I told him I had eaten at a good restaurant the last time I had visited Sechelt. It was about 2:00 p.m. by then and my stomach growled at the thought of food. "Come and show me the way," said the man, "and I'll buy you lunch."

As we walked along the streets, people were pointing or giving shy little waves at my companion. One man even screeched his car to a halt and yelled, "Hey, Bill!" out of the window. I remarked to him that he must be very well known; he modestly said he'd been on TV for a while but the show hadn't done very well.

We had a marvellous lunch and a very interesting conversation. The man commented rather sadly that he'd just had to move to a microscopic apartment that was only 380 square feet—exactly the size of my new cabin. But my cabin does not seem small because I also live in the vast space surrounding it. How people can stay sane with dozens of folk only a wall-, floor- or ceiling-width away never fails to amaze me.

All during the meal, people were staring and covertly pointing, and when this mysterious man went to the washroom, I hurriedly looked through the festival brochure to see who he was. His name was Bill Richardson and he hosts a show on CBC Radio in the afternoons, called *Richardson's Roundup*. Of course I'd heard of him. He is as well known now as Peter Gzowski was when I used to write letters to his program. But although I'm aware of Bill Richardson's show, I've never heard it because it is broadcast in the afternoons when I cannot get radio reception.

Bill spoke that evening and introduced his latest book, *Scorned and Beloved*, a collection of written portraits of "characters" he'd met on his travels, illustrated in a very droll way.

One of the reviews about my latest book, *Nuk Tessli: The Life of a Wilderness Dweller*, criticized my treatment of the people mentioned in it. I would "give the reader a tantalizing glimpse of someone," the reviewer wrote, "then fail to develop the character."

The trouble is, I live with the people I write about. Experience has shown me that no matter how innocuous a portrait I paint, the subject will find something about which he or she is unhappy. The only way I will ever be able to use the same freedom with people that I apply to a landscape is if they live clear across the country or are dead.

Another speaker at the festival was Arthur Black, the man who had interviewed me in Edmonton while I was on the book tour. It was great to meet him face to face. What a shame I can never hear these people on the radio at home. I'll really have to invest in a short-wave set one day.

I had brought Taya with me to the festival (Max stayed home with Hisako). Taya has become very mellow in her old age and her big, fluffy teddy-bear image is always a crowd-drawer. I tied her near the main doors of the building housing the bookstore where thousands of people could see her, and as I suspected, she stole the show. I bet I sold dozens of books on her account. Taya took it all very placidly. People were disappointed that she did little but sleep. So I had to schedule photo sessions and put on her pack and make her sit up and look alert—the only way to do that was with cookies!

The weather was mostly good for the hike in with Matt. Severe bugs the first day, but windy, patchy cloud and a perfect temperature the next. The flower meadows on the big plateau this side of Fish Lake were at their best—they usually peak in late July, so that is extremely late.

All the way across the plateau we encountered dollops of fresh horse manure, and at Octopus Lake, Bob Cohen, the guide for the outfitter, was camped by his tipsy old cabin with quite a crowd of friends. Naturally we stopped to have coffee and chomp on some of the huge rainbow trout they'd caught off my bridge. Apparently the hole underneath it has some really great fish in it: I'm going to have to put a tollbooth on the bridge and start charging a fee! Oddly enough, the higher you go in this country, the bigger the fish are. When the lake survey was done a couple of years ago, this pattern was evident everywhere. Even Cohen Lake, directly above mine and separated by only 100 m of river, has larger fish. Down on Banana Lake the fish are smaller. The only explanation the fish biologists could come up with was that the lower down the fish were, the more parasites they had. It can't be anything to do with overfishing on the fly-in lakes (which are mostly the lower ones), because hardly anyone fishes in mine.

We hadn't been sitting at Bob's camp for long before four big, oldish, scruffy-looking guys walked in. It was none other than the Mike Swayne/Jack Rollo crowd on their annual Alplands excursion. (Remember Mean Jack, who spoke that

execrable German to you?) They towed home, by canoe, the mar-
vellously twisted post that now supports the east end of the porch.
They have been coming into the area every year since before I was
in the country, and they often take a pass by my cabin. They
belong to a club in Seattle that combines high-altitude fishing
with hiking. They'd told me by letter that this time they were
going to be in the McLinchy, a lake south of mine, and I did not
expect to see them. But the fishing in the McLinchy had been so
poor that they had headed to Octopus Lake, intending to go back
down to the McLinchy to fly out. They had no idea Bob was
camping up there, let alone that I would be visiting on my way
home as well. It really was bizarre. Apart from Hisako, and who-
ever might be way down below at the fishing lodge on the north
branch of Whitton Creek, we were probably the only people in
the whole of the Charlotte Alplands at that point—and we all
met at Octopus Lake. The Swayne crowd are old hands at the
spotted dick routine and the thought of it convinced them to
change their plans and come down to my place instead of returning to the McLinchy. I would be able to call the float plane company on the radiophone and reschedule their flight. As always,
they were a hoot to have around, and they bought lots of copies
of the new book, so I did well financially. I also got in a free
Beaverload of freight on their pickup plane, which was an added
bonus.

Since Max has been playing with Hisako's dog, his leg is worse. I talked to a vet at the festival and he says it is probably a stretched ligament. This apparently often happens with big dogs, and because they put a lot of strain on the other leg, that one is also likely to go. It can be fixed but is of course very expensive, and Max may never be able to pack or do long walks again. I shall have to make a decision about him when I go out in the fall.

Today I have been on a writing binge so that I can ship out a bunch of letters when Hisako and Matt fly out next week. But it's time to sign off and make Matt his special reward for hauling all that firewood—yet another edition of the famous spotted dick.

Love
Chris

Max

"Great hospitality—and filling Spotted Dick!"
—Wendy Hooke, Nuk Tessli guest book, 1997

5th Oct 99

Dear Nick,

At some point I am going to have to move the electrical system into the new cabin. Not that the building is anywhere near to being an office working environment yet—far from it—but the cables that connect the solar panels to the batteries currently run under the walls of Cabin Two, and will have to do the same for Cabin Three: it will be a lot easier to shift them if I don't have to dig everything out from under a couple of metres of snow. The trouble is, I still don't know if I will be able to move in myself. I have run out of materials—cement and fibreglass insulation, mainly. Without these I cannot do the stove surround or insulate the floor, and may be able to only partially insulate the walls. By shovelling snow to block the basement drafts and by using extra firewood and clothes, I could survive the winter with the job only half-done. But because I could not line the walls or put the floorboards down, I would not be able to build the counters, cupboards and shelves. It would mean spending the winter with plastic-covered pink walls, using the outdoor folding chairs and tables as furniture, and sleeping on the particleboard sub-floor. I've lived under worse conditions; it would at least be warm and dry—it just wouldn't be very pretty. Buying the cement and insulation when I am out doing the craft fairs next month and flying them in when I come home at Christmas is not an option, for the little Cessna 180, which is the only aircraft the float plane company puts on skis in winter, will not hold very much. I couldn't possibly afford to pay $180 just to fly in a single bale of fibreglass. Any sort of move is tempting, though, for while I have been working, the views of Mount Monarch through the window that faces up the lake have been stunning. Trouble is, if I don't move, I still need the electrical system in Cabin Two, so you can understand why I am in a dither about it.

Australian Matt built half the ceiling before he left. The boards that had been stored up there (the ones Liz and Paul hauled on the ice last winter) had been sitting loosely on the joists; they first had to be jammed somehow into the door end of the attic, and that made it very difficult to move around. The skinny one-by-three tongue-and-groove was actually quite easy to handle, although it took a lot of nailing. Although most of it had sprung into all sorts of curves, all but the most extreme pieces were supple enough to force straight again. It makes a very attractive ceiling. Above it, two-by-fours (real ones, unplaned) were placed on edge for spacers, and fibreglass was stuffed in between. One-by-tens on top completed the attic floor. At once, all the boards were shoved over to that end of the attic, and quite a lot of the lumber still stored downstairs was also piled there. Unfortunately (for me!) Matt did not have time to do the other half of the floor before he left. He claimed to have had no carpentering experience before, but he was a fast and neat worker and he did a really good job.

He and Hisako were due to fly out on the 29th of August. Their plane was supposed to come at around 10 a.m., but when we woke, the previous night's rain had turned to snow and there were 10 cm of it on the ground. This surprised me, as there had been no heavy frosts, but I guess the rains had cooled the earth sufficiently for the snow to accumulate. It was exceedingly sloppy and slippery, and as I was expecting a stove and some other heavy stuff to come in on the plane, I shovelled the sidewalk. Snow has fallen here in August on occasion but I've never shovelled it at that time of year before. The weather cleared around noon but there was such a backlog of clients waiting in the float plane office that our plane never came until about 6:00 p.m.

After that, however, the weather switched and we ended up having the most glorious fall. Hard frosts, mist on the lake, brilliant sun and brilliant, newly white mountains. Four days after the snowfall I hosted a bus tour and was able to show the visitors, to their utter amazement (for it was T-shirt weather by then), a little pile of ice still lying under the eaves on the shady side of the cabin where it had dumped from the roof.

On one of the bus tour planes came a message to say that Janis and his girlfriend Isi were hiking in. What good news to hear that Janis is mobile again after being paralyzed and in hospital last winter. The hike from the road takes two days if you move reasonably quickly; three if you take your time or have to walk the whole of the logging road. The weather was splendid so I was not worried on that account, but when the two hikers had not turned up by the fourth morning, I phoned the float plane company to see what was happening. I learned that Janis and Isi had cancelled their trip.

A day or two later I received another message to the effect that they were setting off on the 9th of September. But once again four days went by and they did not appear. I phoned out and found that the hikers had indeed left as scheduled this time but hadn't known if they would be able to hitch a ride on the logging road to Charlotte Lake, so I allowed them an extra day for that. They finally turned up on day five. Apparently Janis's paralyzed leg had not been functioning 100% and they had taken things slowly.

And isn't Isi wonderful? What a change in Janis! He washes his clothes! He gets up early! Isi is an excellent cook and she introduced a lot of new dishes to the menu. Janis tells me the latest prognosis for his long history of mysterious diseases is multiple sclerosis and the only medication that has been known to help is a heavy intake of vitamins and minerals. He's also on a strict vegetarian diet and that has been a bit difficult to cater to: apart from a few nibbles in my garden patches and the sprouts I grow all the time, I don't have all that much fresh food in here. It is getting to the time of year when good-keeping varieties of vegetables can be bought, but I cannot just go to the store and grab some. Mary and her neighbours are great at shopping in Anahim for me when I need it, but they can't send anything in unless a plane is due. Besides, the vegetables there are hardly "fresh," being your classic Californian chemical products that have already spent many days on the road travelling via Edmonton, of all places (apparently coastal shipping companies are not as reliable). If Janis had warned me of his dietary requirements well in advance, I would have had extra produce flown in on one of the bus tour planes. As it was, I eked out the remaining carrots, onions and cabbage with canned tomatoes, mushrooms and beans. One day Janis and Isi said they'd like to do the cooking. They made a marvellous stir-fry but used up every last scrap of fresh food. "How nice it is to have a real vegetable meal," Janis stated. I agreed with him, but then I told him there would be no more fresh food for the next month. He was absolutely devastated. It never occurred to either him or Isi to wonder how the food got here.

When you ask what Janis and Isi did during their three-week stay, it doesn't sound like much, but they worked incredibly hard. Basically they moved stuff. There was a little firewood to bring home—I'm still enjoying the huge pile of stovewood that Janis split—and a chunk of Ellen's brush pile to stack in the porch for winter kindling. Then there were the remaining boards still stored in Cabin Two; they had to be moved into Cabin Three's attic and the big pile of floorboards that Janis cut last year, which have been sitting all this while on the floor joists in Cabin Three, had to be put into Cabin Two. As they were over 6 m long, the art supplies cupboard under the

Janis

computer had to be dismantled so the ends of the boards could be slid into the space. Then there were the thousands of little one-by-three tongue-and-grooves to move from the upstairs porch (where I had initially put them and where we had to crawl over them to get into the attic) into the attic itself—but first I had to finish the other half of Matt's floor.

With that done, I was really anxious to get on with the stone oven, but it was so cold in the main room of the cabin with the wind whistling though the window hole, even though a tarp was nailed over it, that I decided to finish the windows first. The two larger window holes are each 2 m wide. It would have been great to have nothing but glass in them, but flying in such large double-glazed sheets would have been very difficult, and lifting them into place would have defeated me. So I divided each window into three. Williams Lake Glass delivers to Bella Coola once or twice a month, so Doug Neufeld, the owner, was able to drop the panels off at the float plane company's wharf. One unit was smashed when it arrived at Nuk Tessli—I could hear the glass tinkling inside before I opened the package. Fortunately it was one of the bay window panels, so less important for keeping the weather out at this stage. I phoned out and ordered a replacement; in the meantime, I slipped carrying one of the units and gave it a whack. When I unwrapped it I could see no sign of a crack, but after it was put up, I noticed a tiny glitter of sun near the top left corner. And with every hammer blow close by, the crack spread until it cut right across the pane, so that is another one that will have to be replaced. But finances dictate that I shall have to live with it for the time being. What a difference to the temperature of the room once the Monarch window was in. And right away the blackflies and an inordinate number of painted lady butterflies became trapped against it.

Did I tell you about Doug's adventure on one of his delivery trips to Bella Coola? He was on his way home, in the winter, in the dark, and had just started up The Hill when a boulder bounced down the cliff and through his truck window, smashing the glass and breaking his wrist. Naturally he jerked his arms; the road was single-lane right there and when he came to his senses again he realized he was close to the edge of the dropoff with the vehicle's rear end pointing over the void and his headlights illuminating the cliff. He decided he'd better get out and see if he needed to put the truck into four-wheel drive. His left hand was useless so he reached over with his right to open the door. As he moved out of the truck, he felt it begin to go. His leg was caught by the door and both he and the vehicle somersaulted twenty feet down the almost vertical slope, when he was fortunately thrown clear. His vehicle continued its descent. He blacked out again but, despite a useless left arm and badly twisted right knee, was able to crawl back up to the road. He doesn't remember all of it except that he found himself sitting up there and trembling like a leaf. A car came by right away—the driver had been drinking since Williams Lake and consumed several more cans of beer as they drove, which wasn't making Doug feel any better—and he was taken to the hospital and kept overnight. Having no vehicle to drive home, he flew back to Williams Lake with Gideon, who operates a scheduled flight in a Beaver. As they travelled over the accident site, Gideon decided they should take a closer look and get some photos. So there was poor Doug, in pain and doped to the eyeballs, having to sit in an aircraft that was standing on one wing and doing circles in the Young Creek Canyon over the site of his near demise. You know those goofy T-shirts with the slogan: "I Survived the Bella Coola Highway"? Doug's sister took a picture of the truck, which looks like a mangled ball of aluminum foil, and had it printed onto a T-shirt that says: "I Survived the Bella Coola Highway—But My Truck Didn't." He has the T-shirt hanging on the wall of his shop in Williams Lake next to the photograph.

Janis and Isi continued to move things. Two canoeloads of sand were hauled from the little beaches scattered around the lake—even if I cannot finish the cement work until June next year, I still need the sand brought now, because in spring the water will be so high the beaches will be covered. The sand was quite wet and it was shovelled onto a sloping tarp just above

Cabin Three's little wharf-to-be. More tarps, anchored with lumps of wood, were placed on top. That way the sand can drain and dry, and also remain free of debris and additional soakings until I need it.

Then there were the iron stoves to move. The summer stove from Cabin Two was shifted onto the stone platform built for it next to the oven in Cabin Three, and the heater that was flown in on Hisako's plane is now in Cabin Two. Because the heater is such a different shape, the barrel stove had to be shifted as well. All this activity meant a complete restructuring of the stovepipes, which involved lots of frustrated fiddling around with elbows, T-junctions and hacksaws. The old stovepipe oven was ditched and the only working ovens I now possess are the barrel stove with its firebrick lining, and the outdoor heap of stones.

One day some more surprise visitors arrived for a day hike. I was in dirty work clothes (covered with cement) and was also in the middle of baking bread. As I had lit the outdoor stone oven earlier that morning, I had dislodged one of the roof rocks and it was now hanging precariously into the oven space. Janis is no stranger to breadmaking so I was not worried about leaving him to deal with the bread while I took the hikers up to the lookout. I warned him to be careful about the loose rock in the oven.

We arrived home just before the visitors' plane was due, to find that when Janis was manoeuvring the loaves into it, the oven had collapsed. One loaf was completely smashed—flat as a board. But the other looked great when I had brushed the sand off it— mind you, there was a definite crunchy feeling in the teeth when we ate it. The visitors enjoyed it, too (we didn't tell them about the sand). This little accident meant that more bread was required right away, so as soon as the plane had left we found a much better roof rock and the three of us dragged it with ropes, on planks, to get it to the oven. Now it bakes even better than before.

Finally I could tackle the indoor stone stove. Uli's expensive soapstone monolith has all sorts of channels built into it so that the smoke travels through a complicated warren of passageways. This ensures that it relinquishes the maximum amount of its heat before it reaches the chimney. But my constructional abilities limited me to a simple box with a stovepipe coming out of one end. I had found two suitable rocks to bridge the gap across the top, but was not altogether sure if they would survive the fire without cracking. So when I last passed through Williams Lake, I had picked up several lengths of angle iron to serve as mini-ceiling joists.

They could not lie parallel, as the wall tops were very irregular, but they supported the roof rocks well enough. The spaces between were filled with smaller stones, but sloppy cement would filter through quite tiny gaps so I stuffed aluminum foil into every little crack. The top of the oven was eventually built up to a thickness of about 30 cm, and when I was arranging the rocks I managed to find suitable ones to make a really good flat surface. But when I took it apart and added cement to the equation, things did not seem to fit in quite the same way. I'd had virtually no experience with concrete before, so this was all a big experiment. The biggest mistake was trying to do all of the top at once so that when the cement dried, it shrunk unevenly, and now the nice level stones tip at all angles. The surround on the floor is still to finish and when I next get around to mixing cement I can level out some of the spaces on top. But it doesn't have the quality of finish I had hoped for. And unlike a wooden structure, I cannot take it apart and start again. The chimney is composed of standard piping as far as the ceiling, but those horrendously expensive insulated sections run through the attic and out onto the roof. All the holes in the roof had to be cut, including the one in the metal sheeting, and that was a real pain as my only tools were tinsnips and a hacksaw.

I figured a couple of weeks would be long enough to cure the cement. However, although it looked perfectly dry on the outside, as soon as I put a fire in the oven and the stones started to heat up, steamy water began to ooze out of some of the joints. Then, to my absolute horror, a great crack appeared in one corner. I had visions of rocks too hot to handle tumbling in a heap onto the wooden joists and burning the whole place down. With great trepidation I tried wriggling the cracked corner, but I could not move it. Later, as the stove cooled, the crack all but disappeared. I've come to the conclusion that it is caused by the angle-iron roof supports expanding, when heated, at a different rate than the rock; the walls are thus pushed apart. Ideally the roof of the firebox would have been arched, but when I built the thing I didn't think I would be capable of making it that way. Having completed it, I now think an arch would be quite easy to do and if I ever make another (ha ha!) that is the way I will go. Fortunately the crack is in the least visible corner of the stove, so is not too noticeable.

I'd heard that cement wasn't good for an oven but no one could tell me why. Now, as the stove heated up, the reason manifested itself. Where the rocks were big enough to run right through the walls, heat started radiating from them within a short time, and after the fire had been going an hour or so, some of them were almost too hot to touch. But where cement blocked the heat, the outside remained completely cold. In other words, cement has virtually no heat-radiating powers at all. I'd read somewhere that if you build a concrete floor the sun will warm it during the day and it will radiate heat back into the building at night, but I don't see how that can work.* The heat emanated from the bigger rocks for almost two days after the fire was put out, so as long as the stove holds together, it will do the job it was designed for very well.

After I used the same amount of wood I would have burned in the outdoor oven, the bread was cooked, but only just. I shall need to bake again soon and I'll try lighting a fire the night before to get a preliminary warming of the stones. Seems a big waste of wood, as it is cold enough to need the stove in Cabin Two as well, but better to experiment a bit now, before I rely on the new oven full-time.

About two weeks into their visit, Janis and Isi planned a hike to Wilderness Lake. I suggested they take one canoe to the usual trailhead so that it would be there when they came down, and go with the other to the top end of Cohen Lake, and walk over Flattop Mountain to reach Wilderness. They planned to be away for three nights. The trip could easily be done in less time but they hoped to spend an extra night on top of one of the peaks. After all the gorgeous weather we'd had, it was inevitable that they should pick a storm for their journey.

*I've since been told that for concrete to be an efficient heat conductor, the sand used in the mix must be very fine and the whole should be vibrated to eliminate air space.

Their first day wasn't too bad, although streaky cloud sneaked in from the west. The following day was incredibly windy and during the dark hours they were deluged with rain. On the third day it still rained some and the wind blew severely for a while, but all of a sudden it grew calm and very dark and ominously still. I knew exactly what was going to happen: sure enough, after a small puff of air from the opposite direction, it started to dump wet, sloppy snow. Janis and Isi should have been home that night; they didn't turn up. This time they were definitely overdue.

It poured snow all night—there is no other way to describe it. The following morning 20 cm lay on the ground. I figured that the hikers must have made it to Octopus Lake, been caught by the snow, and decided to hole up in the old trap cabin for the night. If they had done that, they should have made it down to my lake by mid-morning on day five, when the weather, though still dull, was clear. But by noon they still had not materialized. I imagined Janis's bad leg letting him down on the windy climb up the mountain, or the paralysis taking hold of him again, or something equally horrible. So I called the float plane company and initiated a search. I knew that normally the Search and Rescue wait twenty-four hours before looking for people, but Janis's potential health problems made the situation more serious and the weather looked as though it was going to deteriorate again. I also knew Isi had never experienced trackless bush before, so wouldn't know what to do in an emergency.

All the float plane company's aircraft were occupied, so nothing could be done for a couple of hours, and Nimpo Nick was in Vancouver. I kept shuttling back and forth between the new wharf-to-be, where I had an uninterrupted view up the lake, and the radiophone. I was finally informed that an RCMP officer was waiting at the float plane company's dock for a pilot to pick him up at 2:00 p.m. for an initial fly-around. I could determine the planes' movements by their call signs, and eventually heard the pilot announce that he was about to land at Nimpo. I ran out to the new wharf again and looked up the lake. It is difficult to pick out a canoe on the water's surface a couple of kilometres away, even with binoculars, but I thought I could see something among the waves. I ran back to the radiophone and informed the float plane company to wait for a moment; by the time I looked again I could distinguish the movements of arms rising and falling with the paddles. What a relief. I expect everyone was pretty annoyed at my alarums and excursions, but at least we stopped the search before a lot of time and money had been wasted.

Would you believe that Janis and Isi had reached Octopus Lake at about 2:00 p.m. the previous day, before it even started snowing, and simply could not find the trail down? It was socked in up there, and I know that country is confusing with other lakes and inlets and puddles and ponds, but they were definitely on the right bit of water. They actually found Bob's canoe and paddled around all the convolutions of the shore, but still could not see the bridge. I can understand Isi not knowing what to look for, as the bridge is tucked out of the way and the two logs might easily be confused with driftwood, but Janis has been over that bridge six different times. His poor vision could only partially be blamed for his missing it; as he told me later, when he had gone there with other people, he simply let them find the way and took no notice at all of where he was going. (Just like me when I am being driven around in a city.) Janis and Isi didn't find the trap cabin, as that is quite hidden, and eventually pitched a tent and spent a miserable night worrying. The following morning they were presented with ankle-deep snow, which changes the look of everything, and they wandered round in circles until by chance they hit the trail some distance above the bridge and then ran down to my lake in an hour. I was quite angry with them for treating the whole thing so casually. Janis seemed quite complacent when he was told about the incipient search—it was almost as though he expected it as his right. When I lectured him about it, Janis said, "But I didn't know I was going to get lost." If that's not a classic statement, I don't know what is.

Well, here I was being cross with them and the poor things were still sitting in the canoe, soaking wet and exhausted. So I told them to find dry clothes and I cooked them a huge dinner right away. Have you ever seen Isi eat? All you Germans can put away pretty hefty meals—and I certainly don't begrudge you the food after all the work you do—but I have never seen anyone consume food like Isi. She's so slender, but she must be completely hollow. A couple of hours later, it was my suppertime and I asked the guys how much they wanted to eat. Janis looked puzzled. "Just the usual," he said. So I cooked another huge dinner and that disappeared as well.

The very next morning was a moonset/sunrise—and the sky was absolutely clear. With the fresh snow everywhere, it was going to be a beauty. I would have happily let Janis and Isi sleep in to recover from their ordeal, but I could not allow them to miss what might well be the most spectacular sunrise of the millennium. So we jumped into the canoe and went to "Sunrise Lookout" at the back of the lake. Because the lagoon is sheltered by Crescent Island there, the water is almost always mirror calm, even when the main part of the lake is rippled. Consequently the reflections of the moon setting over the blood red mountains, all freshly painted with snow, and with an ethereal mist rising from the water, were fabulous.

Before they left on their hike, Janis and Isi helped me prepare the cabin walls for the insulation. First the wall pieces were levered down in their grooves as tightly as they would go, then they were nailed into the uprights. The gap at the top, and any other place where a sliver of light showed, was blocked with scraps of wood or hardware cloth in an effort to exclude rodents from the walls. Mice, and even squirrels, had caused so much damage in Cabin Two that I was determined to foil them right from the start in this building. While the guys were on their hike, I built the wall structure for the root cellar under the floor, dumped in the boxes of sawdust I'd been saving to help insulate it, then laid the subfloor of four-by-eight sheets of particleboard on top of the joists. Suddenly the place was beginning to look more like a room instead of a junk pile. Janis and Isi were due to fly out not long after their hike and I had planned to put the folding table and chairs in the cabin and cook a spotted dick on the stove, which we would eat while we watched the sun go down. But that afternoon there was a short, very violent wind and rain storm. Despite all our hole-blocking efforts, rain absolutely waterfalled through even the invisible gaps between the fillers. The dinner was a washout; but it was just as well that the storm happened then, as I had thought the walls were weatherproof. If I had enclosed them I would not have realized how much damage was being done to the insulation. So I spent an extra day sealing the joints on the outside with window caulking (which was all I had) and building a sort of miniroof over the window to channel off the water pouring down the gable end. I had to cut a slit in a half-log to insert the strip of metal (working on a ladder with the chainsaw held horizontally)—difficult to explain by letter; you'll have to come and see it for yourself. Then I gobbed roof tar over it to seal it. Both types of caulking look messy, but a weatherproof wall is far more important than looks. I'll tidy it up with some proper caulking at a future date. A bit of a weather front seemed to be looming again yesterday and I hoped for another storm so that I could check out the work before I put the insulation in, but by evening the wind had died and the clouds were breaking, and now, about two hours before daylight, the sky is absolutely clear and still again, and the stars are shining like lamps.

You know that I have been keeping bird records for the Royal BC Museum? Well, all summer I kept hearing a funny cry I could not identify. It was a series of about eight identical notes, quite high and rapid, and the nearest thing I could think of was a kestrel. But I could never see anything. The dogs always got excited about it and would run to the shore and look expectantly over the lake, but they never figured it out, either. Then one day I caught a glimpse of an animal running under the new house. It was squirrel-sized, but appeared to have no tail. The glimpse was so unclear I could not be sure, but when I saw it a second time I got a better look. It was a pika, the little animal that lives in rockslides. It, not a bird, was the originator of the strange call. I had no idea pikas lived so far below the treeline. The dogs had often sniffed interestedly at gaps between the rocks, but I assumed they were excited about chipmunks, which also live among the stones. There must be a tremendous network of tunnels and spaces below the cabins. When I cut out a trap door in the subfloor to give me access to the crawl space, I found one of the pika's hay piles. It was right under my stove! His main crop was huckleberry leaves; they were on their stalks and not at all crushed, but dried crisp and loose-looking like plants in a flower arrangement.

The last sliver of moon has risen (holding a distinct, faintly lit full moon in its arms) and now daylight is creeping into the world. Some cloud quilts the sky and is reproduced in the mirror of the lake. It is not yet light enough to see if Monarch is clear. But by the time I do the dishes, have a bath, fetch water and wood and sweep the floor, then have a second breakfast, it will be light enough to begin working. I am going to start nailing the two-by-fours, which will hold the fibreglass batts in place, onto the inside of the fillers today. The two-by-fours will be ripped in half; the first half will be spiked diagonally (this will mean a lot of fitting, as most of the wall pieces don't have a completely flat surface). Nailed to each half-log, the diagonals will make very strong braces to counteract the force of the pounding of the wind. The second halves of the two-by-fours will be nailed horizontally to form the framework on which to fasten the tongue-and-groove. It's all coming together very slowly—but I'm getting there.

Love
Chris

"It's got to be some kind of sausage!"
—Janis Bikos, conversation, 1995

11th Oct 99

Dear Nick,

The whole complexion of my project has changed. More unexpected day visitors arrived yesterday, and I asked the float plane company if they could possibly buy me insulation and cement from the building supply place at Anahim Lake, and send it on the pickup plane. Having almost completed the first layer of wall insulation I have found that the fibreglass has gone further than I initially calculated; so, with the new injection of materials, I will have enough to insulate the whole living space, floor as well as walls, and this means I can build the furniture and move in at some point during the winter. The replacement panel for the bay window also arrived on the plane, so that can be fitted in right away. Still no sign of Uli's three framed windows, though.

Your last letter arrived at the same time—thank you. I have to tell you about another one I received. Among the correspondence from readers who have enjoyed my books, some have commented on a story I wrote in *Nuk Tessli: The Life of a*

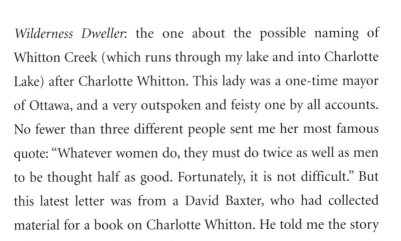

Wilderness Dweller: the one about the possible naming of Whitton Creek (which runs through my lake and into Charlotte Lake) after Charlotte Whitton. This lady was a one-time mayor of Ottawa, and a very outspoken and feisty one by all accounts. No fewer than three different people sent me her most famous quote: "Whatever women do, they must do twice as well as men to be thought half as good. Fortunately, it is not difficult." But this latest letter was from a David Baxter, who had collected material for a book on Charlotte Whitton. He told me the story of how Whitton, having taken office as mayor of Ottawa, had occasion to host the Lord Mayor of London. He wore his chain of office around his neck, and Whitton wore a "smart suit" and a red rose in the lapel. The Lord Mayor remarked, upon seeing the rose, "If I smell your rose, will you blush?" and Whitton replied smartly, "If I pull your chain, will you flush?"

There are two weeks to go before I must leave for the craft fairs and I am getting frantic about trying to get everything done. I figure I will need two days at least to finish putting all the building paper, fibreglass and plastic on the walls, probably two days to insulate the floor (two insulated trap doors have to be designed into the plan: one to give access to the crawl space and the other to the root cellar), two or three more days for the door and its surrounds, another for the cement work still to do and the usual several days' work to shut the place down for the winter. Then there's the electrical system to move over, and something must be done about the door hole in the attic gable end that faces north. When the wind comes from that way, the snow will blow right in. Whether or not I will have time to build a door for the hole I don't know at this point. Maybe I'll just use a tarp or nail on a few boards for the time being. There isn't any floor in that part of the attic yet, just a few untrimmed boards slung over the joists. The new windows need shutters, but I might simply do the board thing with them as well. I only hope the bear that has been hanging around the meadow and causing the dogs to bark a lot at night will not get too nosy when I've gone.

In contrast to the bountiful crop of fruit in Europe that you told me about, we have had no berries at all this year. Even the crowberries are paltry. I've known bad years before, but never one like this. The poor bear in the meadow is no doubt hungry. Having had other experiences with bear break-ins, I imagine him making nice holes in the walls after I have gone. The food and breakables would all be safe in the attic but if Cabin Two's windows were breached, the beautiful floorboards, which I've struggled so hard to keep dry, would be covered with drifting snow and soaked. Fitted under those conditions, they would shrink horribly and great gaps would appear between them.

Nailing in the diagonal two-by-twos meant that I could finally dispense with the last of the braces we had erected to buttress the walls against *nuk tessli*'s furious blasts, and which I have been tripping over for the last year. Fitting the diagonals took so long because all the irregularities on the insides of the fillers (which were numerous, thanks to my inexpert ripping) had to be cut out and chiselled away. Then placing the building paper and first layer of insulation between the diagonals was fiddly because triangles had to be cut to fit the ends.

At this moment (in the dark, but the morning star is high and it will be daylight soon) I am torn between finishing the horrible fibreglass job to get it out of the way, and doing the cement work while the weather is still kind—fairly good frosts in the morning but mild days. I cannot, of course, do cement work if it is too cold, but the building keeps the temperature up, even though there is no door yet in the door hole.

I baked bread in the new indoor stone oven yesterday—successfully this time, and I put a cake in right afterwards. It was interesting to see how much warmth remained in the cabin at the day's end, even with drafts coming through the gaps in the subfloor and a door-sized hole in the north end. What a treat it has been to work and watch the trees toss and sway and the glitter of sunlight on the wind-ripped water, yet still feel calm and warm. What a difference from this time last year, when I was trying to get the metal on the roof and freezing my ears off.

Once again the first pale light of dawn is just beginning to harden the outline of Louise O'Murphy. (The sun rises to the right of her shoulders now so does not appear until a long time after daylight.) Time to do chores so I can get to work. I guess if I got organized and shifted the solar power system over there I could work by electric light...

15th Oct 99

I have a door! It's made from the best of the whitebark boards I cut last winter. A couple of them are from the 500-year-old tree

and are very wide—one is already a bit cupped and it would really be best to rip it so the bend does-n't get worse, but it looks so good I have kept it the full width. Right now I don't have any screws, so ugly nail ends are sticking out of the wood and I'll have to replace them when I get home after the fairs. It's a double door, what we call a Dutch door for some reason

in English, and it's just as well I designed it that way, as it would have been much too heavy for me to fit it in one piece. (The doors for the other two cabins were constructed from store-bought lumber so are much thinner and lighter.) The bottom half was easy enough to hang, as I could support it on the floor while I fitted it. But the top half required me to employ a number of pieces of my body—forehead, elbows, hands, forearms and knees—to hold it while I put the screws in the hinges. I made a few blunders in some of the framing for the door, particularly the part where the tongues of the homemade wooden bolts fit into the door post, so it looks messier than I would wish, but it's a solid door and at the moment fits nice and tightly. The boards have a slight left-hand twist so I hope they will not warp. Even this late in the year, the morning sun shines into the porch and illuminates the door, making a warm spot out of the wind.

20th Oct 99

All kinds of excitement!

It was incredibly spring-like a couple of days ago—not even a frost in the morning. For my decaf break I was sitting, without a coat, on the deck. There was almost no wind and it was wonderfully golden and breathlessly still as only the late fall can be—except for the damn blackflies, which had reappeared for the first time in over two weeks. It's amazing what bad weather those little b——s can survive.

Suddenly I heard an odd kind of moaning. Max at once jumped up and ran along the trail toward the inlet. Lots of huffing and snorting ensued. It was a bear, the one that has been hanging round in the meadow, no doubt, but this time he was just a few metres from the cabin. I couldn't see him but I heard the huffs and moans gradually retreat along the trail. I've never heard one talk so much. It took some time to find the shotgun and shells (even I can't remember where I put them half the time), then I launched the canoe thinking that if I paddled along the shore I might see the bear going along the trail at the head of the first inlet, and scare him off. But when I reached it, Max, who had followed me along the shore, ran back along the trail toward the cabin, so the bear must have been somewhere in between. All this time Taya was asleep. She's pretty deaf these days, so she had not heard the bear and the wind was wrong for her to smell it. However, I figured if the bear got close enough, she would wake up. She's really the bear dog. Max gets all excited and gives a little chase, but soon comes back and doesn't even bark unless Taya is with him.

Anyway, I paddled back to the cabin and all was calm. Taya looked at me sleepily from the new float. Max soon arrived and flopped down on the doorstep while I finished my lunch. I heard him noisily licking his fur, which he often does after he has been in the water, but as I walked out through the door, I realized the whole step was covered in blood. In his excitement, Max had somehow ripped out a dew claw. It didn't seem to bother him a great deal but it sure made a mess.

Just before sundown (an absolute perfect, dreamy evening) Taya decided to stir herself, and the next thing she was barking hysterically in the direction of the swamp as she has done so often this last month. Off streaked Max. There was a tremendous snarling and moaning and huffing and chopping of teeth. I got the shotgun and the bear spray can and went in fear and trembling toward the noise. The bear was up a small tree between Cabin One and the little meadow. It was the first time I had actually seen it: it was very black, even its nose was black. Most of the local bears have a reddish tinge. This critter was obviously just waiting for me to leave for Nimpo so he could make a try for the cabin. Should I shoot or not? I pointed the gun in the general direction and fired. The shotgun can take only one shell at a time so is not the safest weapon with which to tackle a bear. The bear seemed to slump a little and I fled back to the little cabin. Next thing there was a tremendous cracking of sticks and a resumption of snarling and huffing and teeth chopping and barking, and I cautiously went back again—to see the bear in exactly the same place and obviously not a bit fazed by the gunshot. I fired again. Not even a flinch this time, although the moaning and groaning were continuous. I have this theory that bears facing you look large and bears running away look much smaller. They seem really small when they're dead. This one looked pretty close to me but I guess it was too far for the shotgun pellets to reach. The only effect the shooting had was on Taya. As I have now learned, she hates guns as much as she does thunder. Off she ran—she didn't even turn up when I rattled the food dishes at suppertime and I don't know where she hid. So much for my good bear dog.

I obviously wasn't getting anywhere with this animal and the sun had now gone down, so back to the cabin I went, leaving the grumbling bruin up the tree. Max followed me and in his excitement ran into the house, which he doesn't normally do. I wouldn't have minded this time but his foot was bleeding copiously again, so I now have bloody paw marks all over the floor that won't completely scrub off—another incentive for the bear to enjoy the delectable fruits of my abode. I phoned to Nimpo and told anyone who would listen about the bear in case any of the hunters felt like coming out and shooting one, but in fact there has been no sign or sound of the animal since then. I find it hard to believe but maybe the shots scared it away.

Yesterday I did something I did not expect to do this fall: I started fitting the inner siding on the walls. I began against the door post and did the section around what will be the kitchen window. The sun sets over Migma Mountain now and its orange-gold light shone right on that part of the wall while I worked.

I was able to do that because I've finally finished the floor. Unplaned two-by-fours were nailed on edge on top of the sub-floor, fibreglass was put in between and plastic was stapled on top. I've never had the luxury of an insulated floor before, so it will be interesting to see how much difference it makes. I ran out of vapour barrier but had saved the wrappers from the fibreglass batts against just such an eventuality, and by adding a couple of garbage bags I had just enough plastic to seal it. Then, one by one, the beautiful long boards that Janis had cut from the big tree beside what is now the porch, and that he and Isi had squeezed into Cabin Two in September, were dragged out onto the snow in front of the woodshed, edged with a chalkline and hand-held chainsaw, trimmed carefully for length, then carried up to the new cabin. (How much lighter they are now than when we first tried to move them!) The 60 cm width translated to more like 40 cm by the time all the bumps and kinks were cut off. The stone surround for the stove had been built to where the floor level would be and the boards that butted against it had to be fitted to all the small irregularities, which was a pretty fiddly process but they look absolutely wonderful.

In the morning I completed the last of the scheduled chores, which was a door for the attic gable end. I had already done such things as dismantling the float, re-bracing the canoe shed and racking the white canoe, sweeping the chimneys and getting the roof ladder down, and organizing the root cellar in Cabin Two. But I might consider moving the jars and cans to the new root cellar: it's less likely the bear will break into that cabin, as there are no food and cooking smells in it. I would hate to lose my winter's supply of canned fruit—especially the huckleberries from the abundant crop two years back, which I am now jealously rationing because of the lack of fruit this year. The bear might not open the jars, but if he rips the insulation out of the root cellar like the previous perpetrator did, the fruit will freeze and break the glass and be ruined anyway.

I had originally planned to leave on the 22nd of October to give myself plenty of time to prepare for the first craft fair in Prince George, which is scheduled for the beginning of November. But almost everything is ready for it apart from the last minute packing. The handmade block prints were matted, plastic-wrapped and even priced in the spring—I had to wait such a long time at Nimpo for the ice to go in June that I figured I might as well do all that stuff then. I have *Oomingmak* and *Cabin* in boxes at Nimpo, but both *Diary* and *Nuk Tessli* will be shipped by bus and picked up at Williams Lake on my way through. I have to allow a few days' leeway in case the weather is too bad to fly out, but I think I can safely extend my leaving date to the 25th.

The electrical system has still to be shifted. Nimpo Nick has added so many bits to it for the lights, radiophone and charge controller, I'm not at all sure I can get it all apart and together again without some sort of glitch. I'm not sure, either, if the cable from the radiophone antenna is long enough to reach the new cabin. It was so difficult finding exactly the right spot for the antenna before, I don't want to move it if I can avoid doing so at this stage. I will do a computer day tomorrow to get the last of the business mail out of the way, and put everything on disk just in case my computer wipes out in the new millennium, but I'll leave the moving of the electrical system until the last moment.

I have just checked the power indicator on the inverter. When I was writing to you the other morning, I ran out of power. I wasn't sure if it was the loose connection on the solar panels, or because I have been using the electric light so much during these short days. Anyway, the last two nights I have gone back to employing kerosene for the light, and how dark—and stinky—it seems! After two fairly sunny days, however, the batteries seem to be functioning properly again. But I guess it's back to that delightful aroma of coal oil until sometime in February when the days become long and sunny. (Actually, the days in February are the same length as they are now, but they always seems so wonderfully long in the brilliant, blinding spring and so desperately short in the fall.)

21st Oct 99, p.m.

This is really it with the computer! ME day tomorrow. (Moving Electrics!) Wish me luck.

Love
Chris

> *"It was a wartime thing, really, wasn't it?"*
> —Maureen Cavalsky, conversation, 1992

25th Dec 99

Dear Nick,

Christmas Day 1999 and a very special one, as last night I moved into the new cabin. Sort of. I have a plank platform in the bay window with a foamie on it for a bed, and a kitchen counter, a stove and the computer. What more, indeed, could I need? Well, only something to hide the pink fibreglass on the walls and a few shelves and cupboards and things. And books and art materials and food and clothes, all of which are still in Cabin Two. Only a corner of this room is habitable, but by moving into it I can do all the rest of the work without the expense (in firewood terms) of operating two stoves. Living amid sawdust and shavings will hardly be a novelty: all the other cabins I built were moved into long before they were completed.

I surprised myself by managing to change the electrical system over with very little trouble. I colour-coded the wires with bits of wool and drew diagrams to assist me, and everything functioned properly right away. The only thing to cause any real concern was the radiophone. Nimpo Nick and his neighbour Frank Cherne had set it up for me a few years back. It came with an antenna that had to be moved around until the best reception was found. At first Frank sent me up onto Cabin Two's steel roof and I shuffled back and forth astride the ridge cap, holding the antenna aloft like the Statue of Liberty her torch, but the metal caused too much static. Next Nick and Frank walked around the landscape, one person holding the antenna and the other phoning out to Nimpo until the best reception was found. We finally cut off the top of a small tree behind the cabin and tacked the antenna to that. A small hole was drilled through Cabin Two's wall to run the cable through it, and the junction to which the radiophone would be attached was soldered on. The men left everything functioning perfectly, but when I tried to phone out a few days later, nothing happened. Then I noticed Max chewing at something—it was the cable that ran from the antenna tree to the cabin, part of which was lying on the ground. Max has never chewed things very much, not even as a puppy, but he likes to mouth scratchy things like twigs on occasion; the bits of discarded wire, which I had not yet cleaned up, must have been just to his liking and set him off—either that, or Frank and Nick had just been eating hamburgers. I tried splicing the cable the same way you would an ordinary wire, but the radiophone still didn't work. Naturally I could not report the damage until someone flew in, after which Frank and Nick brought in some extra cable and a length of stiff hosepipe to protect it. Apparently the material is coaxial cable, which can be joined only by soldering.

Needless to say, after that debacle I was somewhat apprehensive about moving the antenna by myself. But maybe I wouldn't have to. There was now a lot of excess cable coiled on the antenna tree: perhaps it would be long enough to reach the new cabin. The trouble was, it first had to be gotten out of Cabin Two. The hole that had been drilled for it was only as thick as the cable itself. The attachment that screwed into the radiophone was much larger and had been soldered onto the end of the cable after it had been inserted through the wall. I could not remove it because I had neither the knowledge to take it apart nor the means to solder it back together again. All I could do was auger a much larger hole in the wall, which in itself was not difficult, but I was nervous about damaging the cable while doing so. However, it all came out unscathed and, because I hung the cable on trees (well away from Max's ministrations), I was able to stretch it to its fullest length, and it entered the new cabin with about 15 cm to spare. The phone could be fastened directly beside it but the wires to the solar-charged batteries were too short to reach the floor, so the batteries had to be raised on blocks directly underneath the phone. This would not have mattered greatly but the cables from the solar panels come into the cabin at the other end of the room, where the batteries will eventually sit, and until another solution can be found, these will have to snake across the floor.

The day I arranged to leave for Nimpo, it was snowing—not much, but enough to screw up visibility for flying. I puttered away at the tongue-and-groove in the kitchen corner of Cabin Three, listening on the radiophone to the progress of the planes. They were busy flying hunters north of Nimpo where the weather was a little clearer; there is not much tourist traffic south of the highway in the fall. Late in the afternoon, visibility improved at my end and the float plane company announced they would try and squeeze me in. When the pilot finally arrived, he brought in a large, heavy package. It was Uli's framed windows. I did not have time to look at them as the weather was very dodgy and all kinds of people were stranded, so the pilot was in a great hurry to leave. The air was turbulent and we fell so sharply in an air pocket over the little ridge between my lake and Avalanche Lake that it drove the breath from my body.

I am pleased to say I did quite well at the fairs, but I had some hefty bills to pay. My nice "new" truck devoured a big section of my profits. I had just arrived in Emily's yard at Williams Lake when the transmission went. (I have never owned an automatic before and I never will again.) I was stranded there for two days—and the bill came to $1,100. But what made me maddest was paying $45 for a five-minute tow. A tow all the way from Nimpo Lake to Williams Lake, a four-hour drive, costs only $300. After that I noticed splits in the walls of my tires so bought $400 worth. Then the muffler fell off ($120)—and then I couldn't get out of my Salmon Arm friends' steep, newly snowed-in driveway and had to buy a set of chains for $140.

The other big bill was at the vet's. I decided to have Max's leg operated on rather than have him put down. It cost $900 before follow-up drugs and taxes, and on top of that, Taya also needed attention. Sometime previously I had noticed a lump on her mammary glands, which was obviously a cancer. This had suddenly broken out into sores. The vet said an operation was the only answer, but Taya is at least eleven years old and big dogs don't often live much longer than that. I simply could not afford it. I would have had the vet put her down right then, but after his operation Max had to be kept calm—no jumping in and out of vehicles, no hikes off the lead and suchlike. He is such a wimp with all kinds of vehicles, trucks as well as planes, that the only way I can get him in is if Taya goes first. So I needed her to help me keep him as calm as possible. Taya still eats well and is bright and interested in animal smells, but she now does peculiar things. She lies right out on the lake on moonlit nights, then curls in the dark, shady kennel when the sun shines.

For his operation, Max had his leg completely shaved from ankle to hip. He is unbelievably skinny under all that fur. The leg looked totally out of proportion—as if someone had stuck a scrawny, plucked chicken leg on by mistake. And the hair is growing so slowly. Now, nearly a month after the operation, there is still only a faint peach fuzz covering the naked skin. I thought he might be cold at first, and pulled an old sweatshirt onto the leg when I left him outside. He tolerated it pretty well— I guess he's used to wearing things as he carries a pack all the time. But it was hard to design something that would stay on. Without it, however, he did not seem to notice the cold. In view of both dogs' invalid state, they are allowed inside at night or when the weather is bad. Taya is content to lie wherever I put her mat, but Max has to be tied to the door handle so he can't roam too far into the room.

When I drove back from Williams Lake, Max was doped up to the eyeballs, but he still cried and hyperventilated the whole way. He was so exhausted when we arrived at my "townhouse" (the cabin on Mary's resort at Nimpo Lake) that he could barely walk to the door. I needed to go over to Mary's house to fetch a bucket of water and use the phone and I thought I'd give Max a treat and shut him in the cabin while I was gone. What a disaster! Without Taya inside with him, he panicked. When I came back he had chewed his rope into little bits, also two electric cables (fortunately not plugged in) and several containers already packed for the plane that were sitting on the black couch below the window. Nails and screws, books, jasmine tea, a snow of ripped and masticated cardboard, and waterfalls of oats (fortunately dog oats) flowed over the couch in a kind of macabre potpourri. But worst was the couch itself, which of course is Mary's and not mine. He'd chewed a great hole out of the top, and vinyl flakes and little pieces of foam rubber were mixed with the rest of the stuff. But you couldn't be cross with him because he was obviously so agitated, panting furiously, with his eyes staring. It took him quite a while to calm down.

While I was outside I did the usual round of craft fairs and slide shows, but the big event was an appearance on *In the Company of Women*, a Women's Network TV show that was later broadcast

Canada-wide. The producer had seen me speak at the Sechelt Writers' Festival and asked me if I could get down to Vancouver for the taping. I hate women's gossip shows on principle, but I could not help but like these three women interviewers. It was filmed in front of a "live audience"—a grand total of about a dozen people. When clapping was called for, all the technicians joined in to create a thunderous applause. (I guess I'm not supposed to give away all these trade secrets.) The TV crew ran through about ten minutes of filming, then did it again, and again, with variations. At first they had the usual preconceived city ideas as to what I was and tried to push me in that direction. But I got on my hobby horse to the effect that no, I'm not a wonder woman and no, I'm not running away from the "real" world; and I have to admit that when I saw the final version about two weeks later, I thought it quite well done. And of course, I told the bear-tooth bread pan story. I even had the skull and the bread pan with me. Poor old Taya was there, too, lying by my feet, dopily dozing in the hot lights of the studio. Everyone told me later how attractive I looked. I wore a pink silk blouse, which was thought to be very elegant although some people were quite scandalized when I told them I had bought it on the way through Williams Lake for $1.50 at our very fashionable Salvation Army thrift store. They seemed to think it was sacrilege not to spend proper money on a new outfit for such an occasion. But there was nothing wrong with the blouse; in fact, I probably wouldn't have found a better garment anywhere and I simply don't see the point in spending money on clothes that I would probably never wear again. Part of my "glamour" must be attributed to the makeup girl, who worked on me for half an hour. I was told I would need it to make me look "normal" under the lights. When I saw my face in the bathroom afterwards, I had violent red lips and a green face!

Throughout the interior, where I was travelling for the craft fairs, quite a lot of wet snow and rain fell and it was very mild, so I feared the ice at Nimpo would be no good. But I arrived back there on the 12th of December to find that although it hadn't been cold, there had been very little snow and there were tons of ice everywhere. It took the usual several days to scramble through my obligations at Nimpo: packing freight and doing as much last-minute business as possible by both phone and mail. On the morning of the 17th, I rounded up the sacks and boxes of fruit and vegetables from Mary's house, and a couple of lumps of frozen meat from her freezer, stuffed them into an already over-loaded truck, and drove to the float plane company's hangar. I'd booked the usual two flights, one for me and the dogs and what-ever else we could get in, and one for the most urgent freight, expecting the rest to come in later throughout the winter on pickup planes for all the visitors who have talked about coming.

As the earliest of these are not due until February, I had to plan the arrangement of the freight very carefully. I always put the most important things in the front of the truck and grade them to the least urgent in the back.

Floyd is usually the only pilot around in winter. Sometimes he finds the overflow too deep on his first flight and prefers to wait a day or two for the second; if the weather turns bad in the meantime, it might be a week before the second load can come in. Consequently, I wanted to make sure I had the most important things with me just in case. I knew I needed matches and salt right away, plus, for instance, my down coat in case it got cold. But it was a toss-up whether to bring some of the vegetables or the frozen meat. The vegetables would not all fit in the first plane; if they had to stay in the truck, the vehicle would be driven into the heated hangar overnight. But should that happen and a delay of some days ensue, the frozen meat would not respond well, so I elected to bring the meat with me and leave most of the produce for whenever. One thing that I could not leave behind, however, was the enormous load of Christmas mail, which I was saving, unopened, for the big day. If the second plane did not materialize for a while, I didn't want to be without that.

The weather was mild and vaguely sunny at Nimpo, but we soon flew under the thicker, darker cloud that hovered over the mountains. There was not a scrap of ice on Charlotte Lake (which often doesn't freeze until after Christmas) and it looked very forbidding. It was flecked with whitecaps—there must have been quite a strong wind blowing down there.

Usually Floyd does a test run when he arrives on my lake for the first time in winter. He just brushes his skis over the ice without landing, then checks his tracks for overflow, but this time he landed right away and taxied between the islands toward the cabins. He never gets too close, as the overflow is always worse right by the shore. It looked pristine and white until we stepped onto it—and immediately sank through two layers of partially frozen snow into a slushy soup 20 cm deep. Fortunately I'd thought to throw a tarp into the plane so the freight did not sit right in the water. It was so mild that the snow did not freeze onto the skids, and by revving the motor and rocking the plane back and forth, Floyd was able to break loose and take off.

He decided he could manage the next load right away, so within an hour he was back—and Nimpo Nick was right behind him in his Supercub. Nick had mentioned that he might bring some freight within a day or two, but he never makes a decision about flying until the last minute, and I certainly wasn't expecting him so soon. The sky had lightened just a tad and I suspected the temperature had dropped a fraction of a degree, because this time both planes froze to the ice. Nick grabbed Floyd's wing and rocked the 180 laterally while Floyd gunned the motor, and he was able to get moving that way. But when I tried the same thing for Nick, the Supercub did not budge. It does not have as powerful a motor as the 180 and I did not have Nick's weight and strength. Nick then tied a rope to the tail wheel and got me to haul on that while he revved the motor, then let go so he would have a surge of power to break free. A mighty blizzard of propeller-driven snow flew in my face, but still no luck. In the end, he tried an experiment. He levered the skids forward (that is normally done in the air when the aircraft needs to land on a snow-free runway) and started the plane moving forward on its wheels. He would not be able to get up enough speed to take off on wheels with all that sludgy snow, so he had to try and get the skids back while he was trundling along. From my perspective it looked easy, but he later told me that taking off itself fully occupies two hands and manoeuvring the skids needs a third, so he had to do some pretty fancy juggling to make it work. The Supercub does not hold as much as the 180, so there was still freight left in the truck. Before he left, Nick told me he would bring that, too. After his trouble taking off, however, I did not expect to see him again that day, and the radiophone was disconnected at that point so I could not talk to him—however, within an hour he was back with the last of the freight. All the careful organizing at Nimpo had been unnecessary. But this is the only time all my freight has been delivered right away, and when we started there was no expectation that we would do so, and the planning could not have been avoided.

There was, however, a down side to all of this. On the first day I am home in winter, every step, both on the lake and on the shore, has to be made with snowshoes. By the second day, the trails have packed down and frozen hard. Not only are the snowshoes unnecessary, but also the toboggan slides more easily. Now there was an enormous pile of supplies sitting out on the ice. Could I risk leaving some of it overnight? The produce had to come in or it would freeze, and if the meat was left more than a minute the dogs would have the solstice dinner of their dreams. And although the rest of the freight was sitting on a tarp, there was a risk that it would fall or sink into the water. There was nothing for it, therefore, but to keep plodding, tobogganload by tobogganload, heaving each bag and box up the trail to the cabin. Where are all you strong young guys when I need you most? But the day was very beautiful. The soft, hazy sunshine made everything glow gently, and although Charlotte Lake had been whitecapped, here there was not a breath of wind. After the hubbub of the outside world it was wonderfully silent, and the peace of the place seeped into my soul.

The next day I baked bread in the new cabin, which made it toasty warm, then I scrubbed the floor and slopped on the first of several coats of Varathane. It was dry to the touch after a couple of hours, and in my stocking feet I put in two of Uli's windows, the ones that form the ends of the bay window. (I had stuffed plastic-covered fibreglass into the holes before I went away.) The windows look gorgeous. My original framing was not 100% accurate: minor adjustments were needed, and I have left the third panel (the one that forms an L with the Monarch window) boarded up until I get around to working on that corner of the room. With the sun shining in and the heat from the bread oven, the inside of the cabin was uncomfortably warm, so the first thing I did with the new windows was open them—and open the top half of the Dutch door as well. I then finished panelling the relevant bits of wall and built a kitchen counter and the platform for the bed-cum-seat in the bay window.

Yesterday, on the 24th, I moved in. The big part of that job was dealing with the items that must not freeze—not only the produce brought in on the plane, but also the cans and jars stored in Cabin Two's root cellar. When I left last fall, I wasn't sure which root cellar I would be using through the winter, for the sawdust I had dumped in the new one seemed quite damp. Frozen, it would be useless. But now, when I removed the new, insulated trap door, all seemed dry. The sawdust was for floor insulation only and fibreglass wool would be needed to line the walls. I had almost none of the new fibreglass left, but there was plenty in the old root cellar. First the food was brought over, by toboggan, and piled on the floor, and then I dragged out the old insulation. It was absolutely riddled with mouse droppings, but apart from that, most of it was in surprisingly good shape. I have made a great effort to make the outer walls of this root cellar mouseproof, so I hope for the best.

Moving even those paltry goods occupied all that day and it was right on sundown when I took Max for his last hike on Christmas Eve. (He's not allowed to run free for another month yet and has to have three lead walks daily. Skiing with him pulling and yanking in all directions is out of the question, so I'm gradually breaking trail around the lake on snowshoes, a little bit more every day.)

At this time of year, the sun sets immediately to the left of Monarch, in the very lowest gap between it and the nameless mountains down the Sheemant River. Right around the solstice, when the weather is close to freezing, a curious phenomenon sometimes happens. A ground mist builds over the upper end of the lake, only a metre or two high, and as the sun sets, it pours light into the fog until the upper lake is covered with a rich red-gold blanket, brighter than the very sun itself. The mountains are dark above it and the sky, usually completely clear under these conditions, is quite pale and faintly lemon yellow. I have taken photos at various times but always seem to be in the wrong place for the best effect.

After this extravagant display (in which Max seemed singularly uninterested), instead of taking the icy trail from the lake to the old cabin, I went up to the new one. Even though the old cabin had seemed snug and cheerful that morning, as I walked past it on the ice, it already looked cold and lonely. I found myself feeling unexpectedly sad. It is not as if I was moving more than a few metres. But I have spent a lot of years in that building—more than in any other place in which I've lived—and they have been years filled with hard work, hopes, dreams and triumphs. Nonetheless, I was surprised to feel melancholy.

I was too tired to do much that night, so muddled through supper and stretched out on my new (much wider!) bed. The stars out the window seemed unfamiliar, for although I face much the same way, I get quite a different perspective of the heavens. It is wonderful being surrounded on three sides by

glass. I was woken this morning by the awesome millennium moon streaming over the brilliant snow and making parallelograms of light over the wide, rich floor (and its thick snake of cables from the solar panels). On with the stove and the porridge pot, and I finally started reading the Christmas mail. It would have been nice to have some real people sharing such a special Christmas, but I've often been alone here at this time, and visiting by mail is almost as good as having the person in the room with me. With over fifty letters to read it was like having a party without the mess.

Then out for a while into the lazy warm sunshine with an extra-long midday hike for Max. The temperature was well above freezing and it felt more like May than December. Next thing there was the buzz of a plane and in came Nimpo Nick with one of the (thirteen, I think he said) people staying with him over Christmas. Also in the plane was another bag of mail. Postal delivery to my door on Christmas Day! Among the thirty or so extra letters in that bag was yours.

As I write, the last of the day's light is glowing behind the mountains like some mysterious, distant greenish fire. The air is still, perfectly windless, and just below freezing. The millennium moon is a day past the full so will not rise for an hour, and only the stars prick the velvet sky. The lake stretches calm and pale between the dark humps of land, its secrets locked tight beneath its glittering winter armour.

Now it's the morning of the 27th: somehow yesterday got filled with little chores like putting up a new washing line and tying fat to a tree for the birds (both tasks not at all simple, as they involved the manipulation of ladders, snowshoes, etc.). I also wrote the most urgent replies to my mail in case someone happens to fly by again. It might be weeks before they do, but I always reply to anything important right away, just in case. Today it's back to carpentry work again, so once more I'm in the routine of doing as many of the daily chores as I can before sunup so that I can make the best use of the short daylight hours. Once again, therefore, the moon is high, the stars are a-glitter and the kerosene lamp's yellow flame illuminates the keyboard...

The computer at present sits on a folding table jammed between the stone oven and the door so its cords can reach the inverter, which has to be close to the batteries. When I raise my head from the monitor, instead of the two views I expect to enjoy, and have in fact designed the whole cabin around, all I can see is pink, plastic-covered fibreglass. The computer area is high on my list of things to do but at this moment I need to add more shelves to the kitchen corner. I had thought that what I'd erected before Christmas would be OK for the time being, but there is no space for pots and pans and these are in a muddle on surfaces I need for other things. Remember this when you build your dream home: you can never have too much storage space.

It's been a glorious, springlike week. When the sun shines, I need to open the windows or the door to keep the cabin at a livable temperature. I fear the stone oven was overkill as a heater—I haven't used it yet except to bake bread. Even the small cookstove is let out during the day. So far I am burning a quarter of the wood I would have used in the other cabin. One of Janis and Isi's moving jobs was to fill this porch with firewood. There are less than two cords there and I doubt I will use all the wood during the winter.

And now I will print this off. The reason I wanted to write to you now—apart from sharing my special Christmas with you—is that I must record this and every other file that I have on disk before the new year. Everybody's screaming about this Y2K computer thing. I made inquiries in Vancouver as to whether or not I would have any trouble with my nine-year-old Mac Classic. Some experts said, being an Apple, it will have no problem; others say that because it is so "old," there might be.

It's a bit like Cinderella, isn't it? Will my computer turn into a pumpkin at the stroke of midnight?

We'll just have to wait and see.

Happy New Millennium

Love

Chris

"I appreciate you introducing me to Spotted Dick."
—Glenn Griffin, Nuk Tessli guest book, 1999

16th Feb 00

Dear Nick,

I got a good chuckle from your latest letter when you described receiving the Christmas box I sent you. I originally wrote "Christmas goodies" on the customs form but the post office person took exception to that and made me itemize the contents. That made me mad, of course, so I deliberately wrote sloppily. Your poor mother, with her inadequate English, trying to read to you over the phone the almost indecipherable ingredients for a spotted dick! I cannot understand your difficulty in being able to buy lard. Don't Germans ever eat pie? I didn't put lard in the package, as I thought it might melt and make a big mess. Lard is just fat and you should be able to get chunks of that from any butcher. All you have to do is warm the fat slowly, strain off the solid bits, pour the remains into a container and you have lard. Pig fat is best—don't Germans eat a lot of pig? And kidney fat is the best of all. When Janis was here and could not eat animal products I made the spotted dick with oil, but it was really rubbery. I have never used butter but I expect it would work well enough.

As you can see, my ancient computer slipped into the new millennium without a hitch. If Apple could program their machines properly ten years ago, why couldn't the other

companies? I think it was just a big scam to make more bucks. Imagine that a single industry could hold the whole world to ransom that way.

Things look a little different around here than they did when I last wrote. The computer corner is finished and I'm sitting where I imagined myself to be since I first had the idea of this cabin. The shelf for the keyboard is at an angle to the room so that on my left I have a perfect view of Louise O'Murphy out the bay window, and to my right a spectacular vista of Mount Monarch and his entourage at the head of the lake. At the moment it is still quite dark but a greenish light outlines Louise O'Murphy, and Monarch is a ghostly shimmer against the western sky.

Before I could move the computer I had to move the batteries, and that meant dealing with the antenna for the radiophone. There was a young whitebark close to the cabin porch that could be trimmed and used for a support in the same way we had done with the tree by Cabin Two, but would reception be adequate there? And if it wasn't, how would I find the best position? I couldn't leave the antenna floating in space somewhere while I ran inside to check the phone. The only thing to do was to have a go. So I lugged snowshoes and ladder to the original tree (the snowshoes go under the bottom rung so the ladder doesn't sink into the snow), levered the antenna off, and carried it to the young whitebark, keeping a very sharp eye on Max to see that he didn't get too interested in the parts of the cable that temporarily lay on the ground. Up with the snowshoe/ladder combination and with my trusty bailer twine I tied the antenna on, as close as possible to where it would go. Branches made it stick out at a bit of an angle but I didn't want to mutilate any trees unnecessarily. Down the ladder I went and I called both the float plane company and the Telus radiophone operator. Reception was a bit crackly but I thought it would do. In fact, once the top of the tree was trimmed, reception was perfect. I felt very pleased with myself for having solved that highly technical problem all by myself, even if it was pure luck. The tree is only a couple of metres from the building so I could run the cable to the eaves, tack it to the wall, and feed it into the building below the seat in the bay window. The excess cable is now coiled out of sight (and out of reach of puppy dog teeth); the batteries have been shifted to a large cupboard not far from the computer; and there are no more solar panel cables lying on the floor for me to trip over.

And here is my reward for all this heavy labour of the last two years. I am about to be presented with yet another classic sunrise. Louise O'Murphy is now a light purplish grey with a pale lemon sky behind. The sky behind Monarch is pink, and any moment now the first light will touch the top—ah, there it is, red as a ruby, as if the sun were shining through smoke: there must be a lot of ice crystals in the air.

There has been hardly any snow this winter—less than half of what fell last year. Minus 30°C temps have been common at night, although they've never been lower. But the sunshine has been incredible. Once there was a four-day fog that iced up the radiophone repeaters and I couldn't even raise Nimpo Lake for a while, let alone the Telus operator. Otherwise, little fronts have come in and puffed a few feeble flakes, but a couple of days later the sky has been diamond clear and the sun brilliant again.

There was, however, one other patch of weather that I was glad to see the back of, even though the sun was shining most of the time. This was a four-day blizzard. About 12 cm of snow had just fallen (by far the largest dump of the winter) and *nuk tessli* had started to puff and snort. The sun was shining brilliantly and the top of the storm was a maelstrom of glittering crystals, but the loose snow blowing off the lake was so thick it was impossible to see more than a few metres beyond the windows. The cabin even trembled slightly in the worst gusts and the howling and booming were so bad that I wore ear protectors to sleep at night (for the wind did not lessen during the dark hours). Tons of snow blew up into the attic through the eaves I have not yet blocked, and eddied into the porch. I may have to design some way of enclosing the porch; glass would be the nicest from an aesthetic point of view, but I can just imagine what would happen with that if a determined bear came around. After four days the wind dropped to more normal levels, but it was a further two days before it had slackened enough to make walking out onto the lake bearable.

There are few winters without a blizzard or two of this magnitude, but this one could not have come at a worse time. The day before was wonderful and warm and springlike, just as it had been since Christmas. But my enjoyment of it was marred because I knew I was going to have to put Taya down. Her cancerous growth had suddenly enlarged rapidly in the new year, and the sores were putrid and weeping. She could no longer lie down comfortably, and she was undoubtedly in a lot of pain. The thought of killing her was bad enough, but I also had to decide

Taya

what to do with her once she was dead. Burying her would be impossible among all these boulders, even if the ground wasn't frozen, so I would have to take her into the bush and let the animals clean up the carcass. With luck, wolves would do the job during the winter, but if they didn't, bears would find her in the spring. A bear can become very possessive of meat, rotten or otherwise, and I would have to choose a spot where no one would be likely to walk in the summer. The big bay way up at the head of the lake on the south side seemed the most practical place to take her. It was well away from any summer hiking routes, and wolf tracks usually go through there in winter.

Unfortunately it was also some distance from the cabins. How was I going to get her up there? It would be cruel to make her walk that far in her condition, and I wouldn't be able to drag her body up the lake if the wind was bad or there was a lot of overflow on the ice. The present ice conditions were as good as they were going to get, so if I was going to dispose of her I should do it soon. But of course a job like that is so horrible I kept putting it off. And then, one afternoon, she looked at me, exhausted and sad, and I knew it was time.

"I'll break a toboggan trail with the snowshoes," I thought, "and if it's still calm in the morning, I'll shoot her then." So Max and I walked up the lake and back in the utterly beautiful, peaceful afternoon. When I got back to the cabin, I knew I couldn't wait for the morning: I would have to shoot Taya right away. I chained Max, got the shotgun, took Taya to the far end of one of the islands out of sight of the cabin, gave her some meat as a treat, and pulled the trigger. I should have put her on the toboggan and dealt with her right away, but I was too upset and couldn't bear to look at her. I ran back to the cabin and bawled my eyes out. That night the wind started. The following morning it was impossible to walk more than a few metres onto the lake. But if Taya was left on the ice and enough snow fell to create a lot of overflow, she would sink into it and freeze and I'd never get her out. So I struggled into the screaming wind and blowing snow, dragging the toboggan behind me. Pushing away all thoughts of what she was, I lashed her to the sled, then hauled her onto the island. I tied her to a tree right in the teeth of the wind, where snow would be scoured away and I would not have to dig her free, and there she had to sit for five days. I would hear noises in the night as the storm banged and howled and I imagined her, wounded, trying to drag herself back to the cabin, although I knew in my mind that this was not possible.

When it was finally calm enough to take her up the lake, there was naturally no trace of the trail I had made before the blizzard started. The snow was wind-packed fairly well, but I still fell through into the overflow without snowshoes. I couldn't wait for conditions to improve because they might very well get a lot worse. I put the toboggan rope round my waist and clipped Max's lead to it. He was still having restricted walks and he always yanked and pulled so exhaustingly I figured I might as well put that energy to some use. But of course he rarely pulled in the right direction. When he did, I almost had to run to keep up; otherwise, Taya was a pretty hefty weight, especially as her stiff-frozen limbs stuck beyond the edge of the toboggan and dragged in the snow every step of the way.

Max was supposed to be kept on the lead until the end of January. But about a week beforehand, I slipped on the ice and he got away from me. He tore around like a lunatic for about twenty minutes and then settled down. I figured he had done all the damage he was going to do and left him untied. What a relief that was for both of us. His leg seems to be pretty much OK. He still walks a bit stiffly with it sometimes, but he is never lame after a hike, so he's probably as good as he ever will be. There is still no hair on the leg, and the skin has turned black from exposure to the sun. His other leg has never shown any sign of injury.

At last I could trade the snowshoes for skis and was finally able to go up to Otter Lake. I'd broken trail most of the way, doing just a little bit more every day so Max would not have too much strain on his leg, and in like manner I gradually made a route up the mountain. Now I have trails up to the treeline all over the place.

I more or less finished the interior of this cabin (downstairs) by the end of January. The narrow one-by-three cottonwood tongue-and-groove looks very smart on the walls. There are still bits and pieces to do, mostly fiddly stuff like the facing round the windows, but I decided to leave that until I had finished other chores. Moving all my personal possessions was a tedious job, as the trail between the two cabins has a sharp ascent at the beginning; pulling the toboggan up it was always very hard work. I cannot begin to count the number of times I hauled that sled: a dozen trips were needed for the books alone. And most of the winter's freight still sits in the old cabin: it will go into the new attic and the shelves and storage areas have not been built up there yet. I tried working up there a couple of times but it is far too cold. I need warm, windless days, and you know how unusual that combination is at Nuk Tessli.

The next thing I worked on was the interior of Cabin Two. It was going to be redesigned to sleep five people downstairs. It looked so shabby and smoke-stained when I had ripped everything out that I decided I was going to have to scrub the whole thing, including the ceiling. What a job! The freight had to be packed to one side while I did the first half, then moved back while I did the second. Next I restructured the furniture. The L-shaped bench in front of the windows has been extended, and the whole west side of the cabin is now one single sleeping platform-cum-table. I will have to buy lots of foamies for next year. I once had a letter from someone asking if I rented accommodation by the cabin or the room. A visiting friend suggested I should reply: "No, I rent by the foamie," but I decided I'd better be a bit less facetious to a potential customer.

The summer tourist pattern is shaping up and it looks as though the Grand Housewarming Party will have to take place on the 9th of August. I hope that suits all you guys. One of my trips this year may be in the Rainbow Mountains, the volcanic peaks further north in the Tweedsmuir Park. The outfitters, Joyce and David Dorsey, are offering a horse-supported botanical hike with me as the guide. The clients and I will walk and the horses will carry our gear and food. If this eventuates, it will end on the 4th of August and I will thus be at Nimpo on the 5th to meet anyone who wishes to hike in for the party. Those people who prefer to fly can come on the 8th. Everyone can stay as long as they like, but I have a bus tour to deal with on the 11th, and must prepare for it on the 10th.

I'm going to quit now and continue this later, as the sun has been up for a while now and I cannot bear to be inside any longer. I love that moment when it first peeps over the hill. It is so sharp and clear it almost rings; like a fingernail flicking a wine glass.

Pinnnng. Too nippy to work in the attic, though. Pity; I shall just have to go skiing instead . . .

Next day

The almost full moon is still high and shining brilliantly on the great panorama I can see from my two windows. Minus 30°C again this morning when I trotted along for my morning walk to the outhouse (which is, of course, much further from this cabin than the other: the extra exercise gives me a good appetite for breakfast!)

I nearly forgot to tell you all about the Cariboo/Chilcotin's millennium baby. Although it was not born until the 5th of January, it made TV news. I happen to know the parents because they are Anahim residents.

It was Tamara Lowrie's first baby, and the child started to make his imminent appearance felt late in the evening of the 4th. The nurses at the local clinic were not sure if they could make the two and a half hours' drive to the nearest hospital at Bella Coola before he was born, and they discussed staying put, even though there was no qualified midwife at Anahim. However, the night was calm, with no fresh snow on the switchbacks down The Hill, and it was also comparatively mild at Anahim, being only a few degrees below freezing. It was decided that they might as well set off.

Anahim's regular two-wheel drive ambulance was out of action but the Bella Coola four-wheel drive ambulance had been sent up on loan. The local butcher, who doubles as a volunteer ambulance driver, was alerted, as was his female attendant and the head nurse from the clinic. Father-to-be Paul was invited to join them in the ambulance, but at the last moment he decided to bring a truck—as otherwise his family would have no means of getting back home from the hospital. His own vehicle was low on gas, so he borrowed his brother-in-law's. It was just after midnight when the cavalcade set off. They had travelled for a bit over an hour when the ambulance broke down.

The vehicle pulled over to the side of the road where the sign says "Parking 400 metres" by the little lake just before the East Branch turnoff. The ambulance's alternator had gone, so there was no power to run the lights and heater. Fortunately Paul's truck was equipped with jumper cables, so he was able to feed electricity into the ambulance to keep the lights and heater functioning. It was snowing and windy by this time. The biggest worry was whether there would be enough gas in the truck to keep everyone warm. A comparatively mild winter's night it may have been, but at 1,600 m high in the mountains (exactly the same elevation of my lake), surrounded by ice and falling snow, it was hardly tropical.

And there, perched at the top of the world in their little microcosm of warmth and light, with no other scrap of human occupation for 60 km in any direction, Jeffrey Lowrie was born. He came into the world at 3:00 a.m.; a two-wheel drive ambulance was dispatched from Bella Coola and reached them by 5:00; and as a late dawn was breaking, the party finally entered the hospital. The mother and baby dealt with the situation with great equanimity. So did the father and the ambulance driver— who, after years of volunteer service, had witnessed his very first birth!

Love
Chris

"We used to eat it fried up for breakfast with golden syrup on it."
—Maureen Cavalsky, conversation, 1992

Approx 5th June 00

Dear Nick,

I flew home in a thunderstorm, would you believe! I'm very uncomfortable with flying at the best of times and always like to go as early in the day as possible so I don't have to think about it too long, but it was around two in the afternoon when Mary drove over to my townhouse and told me that Floyd figured it was clear enough to fly. I was amazed, as the thunder was rumbling and banging at that very moment. I was pretty apprehensive about the turbulence but Floyd said as long as we avoided the thunderclouds themselves it would be fine. In the past, whenever I thought it was bumpy, Floyd always said, "That's nothing!" so I wasn't sure what to expect.

However, although we bored through trails of vapour sagging from the clouds, and driving rain streaked the windshield, the flight actually wasn't too bad. I've certainly had many that were worse. When I first came to Nuk Tessli I used to hike home at the beginning of summer but that was always late June, as I was tied up with tree planting until then. Now I always want to travel in as soon as the ice goes. On the way back to Nimpo this year the weather had been cold and clear with good hard frosts and I even entertained ideas of trying to snowshoe back in, but I had to spend the inevitable several days tidying up loose ends, and by then the weather had changed. It rained and thundered and snowed fresh snow on the mountains. So once again my only real option was to fly. I might as well face the fact that I will always have to fly if I want to get home as soon as the ice goes out.

At Nuk Tessli it was back in time again, to tight buds and only the very first hint of green among the earliest deciduous plants. Lots of mountain marsh marigold out in the meadow, but the pussy willows are still tight and silver. Some blackflies but only very few mosquitoes yet, but the pools under the great snowdrifts in the meadow are alive with their jerking larvae. I watch the birds with dread: inevitably, when the barn swallows arrive, the mosquitoes hatch two days later. (The tree swallows have been here awhile; the barn swallows are always the last migrants to arrive.)

This spring I worked for my sculptor friends, Corry Lunn and Darrel Nygaard. They have now opened a studio at Union Bay, which is just south of Courtenay on Vancouver Island. Corry works principally in clay, and in between glazing her unique wall pieces I made several items for myself, most of them experimental. I also managed three large wall sculptures: one was rakued and the other two burnished and pit-fired. The raku plaque was for my dentist—lovely man, he always trades for artwork—and I offered the others, one a study of galloping horses, the other a moose, to a woman in Williams Lake who has bought pieces from me before. (She also breeds Akitas; in fact it was she who gave me Max.) We propped the plaques on the sidewalk in front of her office and it took her about two minutes to decide she wanted both of them, so it was with great relief that I banked her payment and took care of some urgent bills. The spring royalty cheque for *Nuk Tessli: The Life of a Wilderness Dweller* was a considerable disappointment, and if I don't get a reasonable return from the tourist business this summer I'm going to be in trouble. I am still way over my head in debt as a result of having to make payments on the truck.

While I was out, I called our mutual friend Betty Frank and asked her if she had any more dogs like Taya. "Ginger," some kind of descendant of Taya, needed a home. A logging truck driver in Kamloops had taken her to use as a sled dog and breed from her, but he could not keep her because when she was let off the chain, she would run up onto the road into the traffic, and he did not want to keep her tied all the time.

The truck driver was prepared to drive Ginger up to Williams Lake for me, but he wanted to do that on the 22nd of May, and I was waiting for some items to be fired and wouldn't be able to get there until the 23rd. Betty is now living in a senior citizens' apartment (!!!) and could not take the dog overnight, so of course I asked poor long-suffering Emily. When I arrived in her yard it was to find this wild-looking creature shedding great gobs of hair, who screamed instead of barked. Emily herself was not at home but the other people staying there said Ginger had howled all night. She has a ridiculous scraggy curly tail that looks more like a packrat's than a husky's, and which is so lopsided it seems as though it was tacked on wrong. She has a narrow face with a pretty white husky mask and wild, yellow eyes. Apart from that silly tail, she looks like a yellow wolf. She was incredibly hyper and agitated, and tore round and round in circles on her chain, which is not what I want in a dog, but I gave her the benefit of the doubt as she had just been taken from her five two-month-old pups and dumped in this strange place. She was certainly friendly enough with both me and Max right away, and when I slept in the truck next to where the two of them were chained, neither dog made a sound. But it's back to the old yank yank when I take them for a walk. Max was getting to the point where he was quite biddable on his own, but the two dogs together are almost more than I can handle. I didn't dare let them off either in Williams Lake or at Nimpo. Max never comes back when he's called and most sled dogs cannot be trusted with cats and other domestic animals. As we drove past Mary's chicken house to my cabin at Nimpo, Ginger practically leapt through the truck window in her excitement.

She's the first dog I've had that loves vehicles. Max hyperventilates and cries, Sport used to throw up all the time, and Lonesome and Taya merely tolerated them. But Ginger hopped in like this was the best thing since sliced bread and spent the

Ginger

journey either with her nose stuck in the open crack of the window or her head in my lap. I wondered how she'd react to the plane, but once again she scrambled in like it was fun. I kept her tied up for a day at home, but after she had a couple of feeds, I let her off. What excitement all around. I'd made her a dog tag out of a canning jar lid and scratched her name and Mary's phone number on it, just in case she took off, but she showed no intention of doing so. She is very alert and seems extremely intelligent. I was busy with other jobs when I first came but today I put the canoe in the water and went round the northeast edge of the lake. Ginger followed Max, tearing along on the shore, crashing through bushes and falling over rotten logs. She's obviously not used to such rough country and, like all the dogs I've brought here, is exceedingly clumsy at the moment. She will get used to it, though. When we came to the first inlet, Max plunged in to swim across. But no way was Ginger going to get into that water. I canoed to the head of the inlet and she at once realized she could run round the edge. She hardly needed showing for the second inlet and she ran back home her own way, while Max swam, with no hesitation at all. None of my dogs have liked water much, but teaching them the way round the inlets is usually a very lengthy process.

Nimpo Nick was by the other day, on his way to check out the ice on Wilderness Lake. Mary has finally got permission (after two and a half years of negotiations with the Land Office) to put a cabin up there as part of the Nimpo Lake Resort. She had hoped to erect it this month, but even in such an early year, the lake up there is still frozen solid. It's only about 150 m higher than my place but on a much colder branch of Whitton Creek that is fed by several glaciers. Below the confluence where that branch joins the outflow from my lake, the river is always thickly frozen in winter, whereas my branch has lots of open water in all but the very coldest spells.

When I first heard about the cabin proposal I was quite depressed. All the other resorts have put their remote buildings on the lower lakes: the Wilderness Mountain area is one of the wildest and most exciting for hiking and I always felt that it was part of my own "Queendom." But if development has to happen, I'd rather it was for a non-abusive form of tourism than logging or mining. And Mary is at least a year-round local resident. As always when dealing with the wilderness, the big problem is to hit the right balance by providing enough facilities so that people will want to come and support our claims for the integrity of the place without wrecking the country. Now that I am getting used to the idea, I can see a way to incorporate their cabin into my own business for a hut-to-hut hiking tour.

At Nimpo Lake I received your latest letter. How interesting that Ellen has to do a shooting course as part of her forestry degree—but how maddening that her exam is on the 5th of August. Even flying the whole way, from Germany to Vancouver then Anahim then here, she will not make it in time for the party. The horse trip in the Rainbows is now confirmed, so I have to be at Anahim Lake on the 30th of July and will set off here on foot a couple of days before. Hisako is coming in again to house-sit; I shall leave Ginger with her but take Max with me as a pack dog will be useful in the Rainbows, but I'm not sure how Ginger would behave with horses, so it is better that I leave her at home.

I was full of good intentions today—I'd planned to get the Alaskan Mill out and take a board off the chunkiest half-logs that are stacked behind the cabin so I could make a start on the porch walls. The logs are too heavy for me to drag around and lift, otherwise—besides, I can never have too many boards. But a cold wind and spitty bits of rain drove me inside to the warmth of the stove. Now the weather seems to have cleared up a bit so I'll get outside and sow some salad greens and radishes in the top part of my little garden patch. The water is very low everywhere so the runoff has already drained from the upper terrace. The rhubarb shoots are just peeking through like crumpled yellow brains. Low-water years usually mean low-bug years, so here's hoping.

Typical June: the weather cannot seem to make up its mind what it wants to do. Fresh and sunny and breezy one moment, and gloomy and chill the next. This morning the clouds seemed to be clearing, and for a while Monarch and his entourage were gleaming yellow-white and almost clear of clouds, although a heavy grey lid of vapour lay like a slab of chocolate above the lake. The intervening land was dark and the water below was streaked silver with cat's-paws over the gold, grey and almost black reflections. Loons were calling; fox sparrows were singing their clear, sweet song. I long to be up in the mountains exploring, birdwatching, painting, but once again carpentry work takes precedence. But next year...

Love
Chris

"Thanks for sharing your home, your bread,
and your Spotted Dick."
Susan Wilkerson, Nuk Tessli guest book, 1993

7th July 00

Dear Nick,

Six days ago there was nothing but wild, unmarked country up at Wilderness Lake; now a full-sized cabin perches on a little knoll beside the outlet. A bigger contrast to my building opera-tion there could not be.

The ice did not go out up there until the 26th of June. On the 30th I received a message that the project was to take place over the July long weekend: the planes would start to bring stuff in on the 3rd, and if I wanted to be there at the beginning of the pro-ject, I would have to leave home on the 2nd.

A couple of days beforehand, I acquired a new helper. She is a twenty-year-old young woman called Naomi (long blonde hair—you'll meet her at the party!), whose family I've known since she was about three, although I have not seen much of Naomi herself in recent years. She's certainly grown! She was raised in suburban Victoria, but she's quite fit as she's done a lot of sailing. She likes walking but had never backpacked before; the hike into Wilderness Lake turned out to be a pretty good one for her to cut her teeth on.

The day before we wanted to leave, it snowed. Huge, floppy flakes fell from a sky as dark as charcoal and 5 cm accumulated on the ground. On departure day the snow had melted around the cabins but the sky looked so foggy and dreary that we delayed our start until noon. It didn't do us much good because it was soon dumping rain and snow again and we were deluged like that for most of our journey. It was one of the coldest, wettest hikes I've had in a long time.

Whenever I've been into Wilderness Lake before, I've approached it over one or another of the mountains that surround it, and incorporated it in a trip of three or four days. But if I wanted to create a hut-to-hut tour from the Wilderness cabin to mine, the most logical place to put a trail would be directly up the river. The trail that I had already made to hike out to Nimpo could be used as far as Octopus Lake.

I've always canoed across my lake to reach the trailhead, but I'd never yet tried Ginger in a boat, so rather than risk having her flip us over, especially when we were carrying all our gear, we paddled right around the shore and let the dogs run alongside. Ginger ran gaily around the inlets as she was by now in the habit of doing, while Max swam across, but then we came to the river, which Ginger had not encountered before. Max plunged in as usual, but Ginger tore off along the bank, no doubt expecting the water to end at some point; she was gone so long I wondered if she would keep running until she hit Charlotte Lake. Eventually she came back, but although the rest of us were far ahead and calling encouragingly, she would not attempt the few metres of wet stuff that separated us. In the end we went back for her and managed to get her somewhat precariously on top of the packs in the canoe. What with her wriggling and the current pushing us toward the rapids, we nearly tipped before we got across.

The snowy rain had settled in pretty heavily by the time we reached Octopus Lake. We did not cross the bridge, but followed the edge of the lake, figuring that by doing so we would reach the river before very long. Famous last words. I had known that country was confusing, but we must have walked 5 km to cover one. We would scramble through brush and swamps to go round one arm of the lake and promptly find another equally large one in front of us. Some bodies of water had very narrow necks with stepping stones we could cross; others were not connected to the main river system at all. But we could never figure out which it was just by looking, and consequently we had no idea which way we should go round. No mountains were visible in the lowering cloud and the map was no help; not only are most of the ponds not marked, their location is right at the edges of two maps so it is very tricky trying to decide exactly where you are. And all this time we were drenched with the heavy, bitter cold precipitation. Finally we connected with the river proper. For a while it was suddenly very easy going, and very pretty, too, despite the miserable conditions. But all too soon we became embroiled in dense clumps of subalpine fir. The little ridges of land were, for some infuriating reason, all crosswise to our route and we would struggle up one, only to find that we had to drop down again before we could surmount the next.

Wilderness Lake is right on the treeline and faces the prevailing wind. When I'd camped up there before, it had been in good weather, and I couldn't recall if there was anything in the way of shelter for a tent up there. I had no desire to spend the night in an exposed place in these conditions, so we stopped about half a kilometre short of our goal and pitched our tent in a sheltered pocket to the lee of a dense clump of subalpine fir. The majority of the ground was snow-free but there were large, needle-freckled drifts dotted about. We were both too miserably wet and cold to make a fire, so we pulled on dry clothes, crawled into our sleeping bags and ate bread and nuts and water for supper. The following morning was cool and damp with lots of low, misty cloud, but it had at least stopped raining. We cooked breakfast and started to smoke-dry our sodden clothes. If it was like this at Nimpo Lake, no one would be flying anywhere.

But it must have looked better down below, because our socks were barely lukewarm when we heard a plane, and Nimpo Nick's Piper Supercub swooped low overhead, followed by a much larger aircraft. Pete Lafferty and Warren Bean, two of the new owners of the Wilderness Rim Resort at Nimpo Lake, had both volunteered their Beavers for the weekend. We threw our stuff together and half an hour later trudged over the last big snowbank to the shores of Wilderness Lake. The planes had flown out again already, but a group of Nimpo neighbours were clustered on the knoll where the cabin was going to be. The weather was quite pleasant at that point, and Naomi and I festooned the bushes with our clothes and equipment, and were able to dry out pretty well. There is a silvery sandy beach close to the cabin with a dense line of subalpine fir running parallel to it. Behind the fir was a selection of grassy, well-sheltered tent sites: several were covered with a thin film of water this early in the year, but a couple were dry. When the runoff is gone there will be all sorts of places to camp, so my fears about lack of shelter had been unfounded. The ring of nameless mountains and glaciers at the head of the lake peeped in and out of clouds that were beginning to break apart. It was to be the only good weather of the weekend.

The cabin, which is much the same size as mine would be without the bay windows, was constructed of dry western red cedar in a builder's yard in Williams Lake, and it has sat there for the two and a half years it took the paperwork to crawl through the Land Office's convoluted channels. The logs, therefore, were as light as they were going to get. But even so, the longer timbers were too cumbersome for the small planes, and a helicopter was hired to carry these. Nimpo Nick had a heavy-duty scale so was able to bundle the logs into five loads, 700 kg each. They were driven to the closest point along the network of logging roads that radiates out from Nimpo, and about an hour after we had arrived at Wilderness Lake, we heard the familiar *whup whup* of a chopper's rotors. Suddenly there it was, framed between the steep sides of the valley. The first load included the ridgepole, which looked enormous hanging vertically on a long cable below the helicopter. The pilot manoeuvred the bundle of logs to the tiny tundra knoll, and was able to release his load without getting out of his craft. With a graceful swoop, the helicopter leapt away, to return in about an hour with the second bundle. The logs were left undisturbed while the handymen began on the foundations; the rest of us unloaded planes as they arrived and packed the materials up from the sandy beach to the knoll. Trip by trip, the three small planes brought in all the smaller logs; 60 5-metre two-by-fours, 75 5-metre two-by-twelves, 90 3-metre two-by-six tongue-and-grooves, 24 sheets of plywood (ripped in half lengthwise so they would fit inside a Beaver), 20 bales of fibre-

glass insulation, building paper, vapour barrier, a generator, an air compresser, a chainsaw, two skill saws, hammers and drills, and 22 sheets of rolled steel roofing, crated and bolted to a Beaver's float struts.

What we didn't realize until later in the day was that a log had slid out of the second helicopter load and fallen 100 m straight down into a cutblock. Fortunately the log builder, who was operating the truck at the Nimpo end, was able to retrieve it—every single bit of it. It had shattered into a dozen pieces. Each end had broken off at the notch, the main part had snapped in half and it had also split lengthwise several times. To fit a new log would take two days and delay the project beyond the time that most of the planes and personnel would be available. The log builder, however, said he could fix it.

The foundations were built of cedar blocks, two-by-twelves and the half-sheets of plywood, and voila!—by the end of day one, there was a floor.

On day two, the walls were raised. There were enough willing bodies around so that most of the light, dry logs could be lifted manually, especially when the walls were low. Once the window level was reached, the west side of the cabin could proceed independently. While those two corners were being slotted together, the builder collected the shattered fragments of the broken log and proceeded to put them all together. Because of its location a little below the east window, a patch job would not affect the cabin structurally.

The pieces of log were splintered like matchwood. Some of them had become irretrievably sprung and the insides had to be cut away. But all the outside pieces, no matter how small, had been carefully saved. It was like magic. Within minutes, the builder had sliced off a bit here and another bit there, and stuffed fibreglass wool into the holes. Apart from one crack on the outside of the log, which will be epoxied to make it weatherproof, there is no sign of the damage that was done.

Because of the overhanging porch, the longest—and therefore the heaviest—logs went on last. By now, no one could touch the tops of the walls when standing on the floor inside the cabin, let alone outside, so a system of skids was organized. There were about twenty people on site at this point and the logs were raised by all of us working together. Some people pulled on ropes slung over the top wall log, and others shoved with two-by-fours from below. There was no finesse to the operation, simply brute force, and a lot of faces were red with exertion at the end of it. When you and I did the same job at home, the extra loop of the rope around the logs converted them into simple pulleys, so we were able to raise our roof logs with a lot less effort.

The structure for raising the ridgepole, however, was a great deal better than the method I devised. First a scaffold of two-by-fours was built at each gable end. Each scaffold had three steps. A man balanced on the top wall logs at either end, cradling the ridgepole in his arms. Everyone else used two-by-fours and pushed from below. "This is a real Fred Flintstone operation," the builder shouted gleefully as they heaved the ridgepole up the scaffold, one step at a time. It was in place in a matter of seconds.

The weather had been deteriorating all day and by now wind and rain were making the work site very uncomfortable. The crew barely had time to pose for a photo in front of their new structure before piling into the planes and heading down below to home-cooked meals, warm beds and showers, leaving Naomi and me to the elements. Several of the men had originally intended to camp for the weekend, but they had chickened out pretty quickly in this bad weather. There would not have been plane space to ferry Naomi, myself and the two dogs back and forth all the time, so if we wanted to be present for the whole of the operation, we would have to stick it out.

And in the morning it was snowing again. Our tent was dry enough inside, but I was cooking on an open fire on the beach and was getting very fed up with being wet. I hunted around the building site and snaffled a couple of unused half-sheets of plywood and some vapour barrier. With these, I constructed a semi-teepee in front of the fire. There was not a lot of wind at that point—a good puff would have knocked it over—but a small onshore breeze pushed the warmth from the fire into the shelter. It also pushed in all the smoke. Naomi and I drank coffee, did crosswords and improved on our tans—i.e., the leather kind: with smoke, not sun.

Nimpo Nick had left me a radio so that I could give the pilots a weather report. It was midday before I could climb onto the particular rock from which the radio would transmit and tell the pilots that the cloud had lifted enough for them to get in. The first job for the crew when they finally arrived was the roof.

Two-by-twelves were nailed at right angles over the ridgepole to make rafters, then two-by-fours were pounded on for the strapping. The generator was roaring, nail guns were banging, drills and skill saws were whining, planes were coming and going, and the wind was buffetting about our ears. Wilderness Lake wasn't living up to its name too well right then. Late in the day, building paper was laid on the roof and the first sheet of metal was screwed down. There was quite a stiff breeze blowing off the

Wilderness Lake

water and I would have got nowhere doing that job on my own, but with a strong-muscled, experienced crew it was executed very quickly.

Only one side of the roof was in place before the pilots declared that the light was going and those who wanted a proper bed had to leave. My sleeping bag is a good one and toasty warm as long as it is dry, and I decided to sleep in the cabin. I spread my bed on the plywood floor under the covered half of the roof. The gable end facing the lake will eventually be mostly glass, so at the moment it was wide open. Miraculously, the wind died; a few mosquitoes tried their luck, but it was too cold for them to function in more than a desultory way. There was a promising, faint pinkish glow to the heavy greyness of the sky. The lake grew still and the snow-slashed mountains were echoed in its mirror calm. The cabin was like a boat, hanging in the bowl of the lake. Mountain streams swollen with melting snow filled the night with their song.

The long weekend was drawing to a close and this was to be the last day that the two Beavers were available. Nick's Supercub would have needed to make two trips to fly us home; also, I didn't want to risk taking the dogs in his plane. Supercubs have a fabric skin that is stretched tight by heating once it is attached to the frame. One time when Nick flew in to my place during the winter, I asked him to take a gas can out so it could be filled. Instead he offered to decant fuel for me from one of the tanks in the wings. We had no hose, so the gas can was perched on a precarious tower of firewood rounds. At one point these collapsed and a sharp edge ripped a hole in the plane's fabric. A bit of duct tape patched it up, but I could just imagine the kind of damage a struggling dog would do. So when Warren Bean offered Naomi and me a ride home in his plane, we were more than glad to accept. It would have taken us six hours or more to find the way back down to my cabins on foot. The flight took exactly six minutes.

Today I'm drying out and cleaning up, and Naomi is wobbling home in the canoe with loads of firewood from the pile I made during the winter at the head of the second inlet. (This was the wood that was left over from lumber making that Sandra and her Italian friend had split and stacked for me last summer.)

It is another fairly decent day, and as I write I can hear the thin drone of the planes coming and going from Wilderness Lake and wish I could be up there too. The roof and deck will be finished today, and most of the interior carpentry work will be done later. There will eventually be a proper shower inside, a compost toilet, and propane for cooking and heating. They've already got the radio antenna up. Nick dropped by on his way there this morning to pick up the films I exposed. There's nowhere in the

Chilcotin that handles films, so I'm mailing them to Hisako in the hope that she can get them developed and bring them back to us in a couple of weeks when she arrives to house-sit while I am away in the Rainbows. Otherwise I probably wouldn't get to see the pictures until the fall.

28th July 00

A wild storm is blowing itself out (I hope) over the mountains. It is early: the sun is shining for the first time in a couple of days; its light is harsh and brassy. Shreds of black-bellied clouds race from the southwest and a wind drones and beats against the house; the deep grey-blue lake is frothing with whitecaps. Parts of the mountains peep out from a shroud of vapour. But it is a vast improvement from yesterday with its lowering gloom, thrashing wind and heavy rain. We really are having a lousy summer. I hope most fervently that the improvement continues, as Naomi and I plan on leaving for Nimpo first thing in the morning. Hisako is due this afternoon.

I never thought it would be done, but everything is finished. The cabin; three levels of decks; the final bits of carpentry inside; the stone patio under the porch, which includes the great door stone from the boulder I buried (I'm VERY proud of the stonework— I can't wait for you to see it); the new wharf; the attic shelves; the

upper and lower floor for the attic; a door for the interior gable end; the two insulated dog kennels; the horrendously massive cleanup; even the cabin photo album, which was the last job I did yesterday. (The cleanup, I should add, is so well done largely thanks to Naomi. Good thing I had a female helper this year; men never do that kind of thing as well.) You will get a chuckle out of the steps into the attic. I designed them so that I could walk up carrying a bag of dog food (or whatever) on my shoulder. It is very noticeable how my attic steps have evolved over the years. Cabin One's are little more than a ladder; Cabin Two's have much wider rungs, but the angle is still quite sharp; Cabin Three's is a regular staircase. The steps are a visible record of my aging knees.

These last two months have been incredibly focussed: apart from the trip to Wilderness Lake I have done nothing but concentrate on this place. I've had no walks; flowers, birds, full-moon sunrises—all have been abandoned. Still, it's been good to have the deadline, otherwise the work would have dragged on forever.

Mind you, it's not as if work on a place like this is really finished. Maintenance chores are now screaming to be done. Never, NEVER will I EVER build a CABIN AGAIN! (But it seems to me I've said this once or twice before.)

I have little else to tell you. Naomi went on a two-night backpacking trip alone to Anvil Mountain. She took Ginger along and packed her heavily; Ginger did fine. (She goes with everyone, so I knew she would not be likely to run home with Naomi's food on her back, as Max might have done.) The only other item of note was a bear sighting. The dogs constantly gallop off with great suddenness after squirrels, so I was not too concerned when they did it one morning. But a few minutes later they tore off again, this time with a single woof from Max. I heard a crash of brush but could not pinpoint it. The dogs ran along the lakeshore to the place where the shallow rocks almost make a causeway to Big Island, and Max started to swim over, but then he turned round and came back. All seemed calm. But then I saw a tiny dot in the lake, way over the other side of Big Island, heading for the outlet. Even with the binoculars I couldn't make out whether the ears belonged to a bear or a moose, but as the animal climbed out it metamorphosed into a grizzly. He didn't even shake himself, just kept running, long wet hair streaming water, and disappeared into the forest. He hasn't been back, so I assume he has no intention of causing trouble.

Well, I think that rounds up this edition of the saga. I'll be able to give this letter to you in person, rather than mailing it. Save myself the price of a stamp. It's hard to believe that in a couple of weeks you will be here and the party, and all its shenanigans, will be over.

Love
Chris

INTERIM

The Housewarming Party

I had arranged to meet those who were hiking in to the housewarming party at a restaurant at Nimpo Lake on the evening of the 5th of August. We would drive to the trailhead near Charlotte Lake and camp for the night so that we could get a good start in the morning. Four people joined me for supper and three more phoned to say they were on their way; while we were eating, German Nick, Markus and five of their friends arrived together in a van. Many sported earrings and wild hair—garb that no one would think twice about on a college campus but that stood out quite dramatically in Nimpo Lake. Markus was now studying at the University of British Columbia and he had acquired many student friends. This exuberant crowd swelled our hiking numbers to fifteen.

The first time I hiked up Maydoe Creek from Charlotte Lake at the end of the logging road, I didn't know that there had once been a trap trail through there, for there was very little sign of it, and I simply bush-bashed. After several journeys back and forth (I was walking out every month for mail at that time), I linked game trails to bits of the old trap trail, and where it went through swamps I blazed new bypasses of my own. Every time I travelled the route I spent an extra day or two working away at it until it was quite well marked. But mail trips outside are no longer necessary and I now travel the route only once or twice a year. Slide alder and misery bush have grown back with a vengeance, and there are also a lot of new beetle-kill windfalls to make the walking interesting. For someone who does not know where it is, the trail, once again, is virtually impossible to find. Trail maintenance has been long on my "do" list but the summers are short and other things have taken precedence, especially since the cabin project was initiated.

And now I'm not even sure if I want to spruce up the trail through there. The hundreds of hours of work would be of only small benefit to me—but very useful to a great many other people who would be delighted to capitalize on my labour and who might be very harmful to the environment. A couple of years ago, it was proposed that a logging road be built partway up that valley. The road is supposed to be constructed with the environment in mind and then get plowed up and seeded right away, but the country at the lower end of Maydoe Creek is too open to block a road effectively. On the coast, all the logging company has to do is take out a culvert and no one can travel on wheels into the bush any more. But near Charlotte Lake the trees are so widely spaced that a couple of swipes with a chainsaw will make a new way round any kind of barrier, and mushroom pickers, hunters and joyriders will ensure that the road is there for the duration. What is more, they will rapidly expand their avenues of access if they find an easy way through. At present, the rougher part of the bush begins where the logging is supposed to end. If I improve the overgrown part of the trail, it will be hacked into a bike or snow-machine road in no time, and even expanded for a truck if possible, thus giving easy motorized access to the huge, sweeping plateaus of the high country. Most machine recreationists cannot accept the idea that such a harsh and apparently "barren" landscape might be fragile, and they can damage an ecosystem frighteningly quickly. Every time I force my way through the present jungle, I curse and swear at the tangles of windfalls and grasping branches, but it may be necessary to leave the route that way to keep the Charlotte Alplands safe.

All of which meant that my hiking party had quite a difficult time for the first part of our journey back to Nuk Tessli. The weather was uncharacteristically hot, which didn't help; fortunately there are several shallow lakes en route in which we could cool off. German Nick, leading his happy band of adventurers at a tremendous pace, soon got lost in a megaswamp and gave them all a lot of extra exercise. I stayed with the plodders and we all reached the campsite at the head of Maydoe Creek at the same time.

In the best conditions (at the end of summer when the swamps are dry and the creeks easy to cross), I have completed the whole hike to my place in one day. It's only a matter of about 25 km, but the absolute minimum hiking time is fourteen hours. Alone, I usually spend one night out, but with most hikers I prefer to camp twice. This makes the central area, which is all alpine, much more enjoyable. It is also more practical because in the forested parts there are very few tent sites, even for a single camper; anything not sloping and covered in rocks and trees is swamp. The alpine areas can be camped upon only when the weather is not too severe, but the subalpine sections at both ends of the hike are blessed with a number of excellent sites.

A creek gushes out of the mountain directly opposite the campsite at the head of Maydoe Creek. Where the water runs into the forest there is a gorgeous flower garden. Red, yellow, white and purple colourscapes kept me clicking the shutter for hours. The more energetic hikers shot up to the top of the creek and disappeared, eventually returning by sliding down the large snow slope beside it. This snow patch often avalanches quite dramatically in the winter and our tents were pitched among scrubby 150-year-old trees that had been uprooted and pushed several metres during a heavy-snow winter a few years back.

The following day was perfection. No trail at all now, but the going was easier and we climbed up the long, steep slope to a high shelf, traversed Halfway Mountain, dropped to cross a creek, and finally trudged up again to a great plateau, which gave us a panoramic view of the Coast Range. Right in front of us was Wilderness Mountain, but the lake and Mary's new cabin were hidden behind a ridge. Below us, in a sea of forest, were the convoluted appendages of Octopus Lake that had given Naomi and me so much trouble when we tried to find a route through them. The plateau should have been full of flowers but this year there were hardly any blooms at all. This was all the more remarkable because the Rainbows, the volcanic range 60 km north of my place, where I had served as botanical guide the previous week with the local outfitters, had put on the most spectacular display of flowers that the outfitters had ever seen.

About four hours' hike the following day saw us down at my lake, and now there was an interesting little conundrum to solve.

The grand flotilla waiting at the trailhead for fifteen people, fifteen packs and one dog, consisted of precisely two canoes.

German Nick and his cohorts arrived first and Nick paddled across the lake with a load of packs while the rest of the students hiked the extra hour or so to the cabins. There was no trail round that side of the lake, and the bush, being on a north-facing slope, was dank and dense. When my group arrived at the trailhead I could see that the wind was pretty strong; this was going to add more twists to our logistical problems. I took one other person and more packs in the second, smaller canoe. (I didn't want to leave the packs unattended just in case there was an interested bear around.) As we swung out from the little inlet into the lake, we passed Nick, fighting every centimetre of the way, trying to get back to the trailhead. I knew I would never be able to make it up the lake by myself, so, having dropped off my load, I had to return with precious space taken up by another paddler. It was one of those classic mathematical problems in which you have to get people across a river in a small boat with the minimal number of trips.

I had just arrived with my third and last boatload and had not even managed to get out of my filthy, sopping clothes (despite my efforts at fibreglassing, both canoes still leaked), when there was the drone of a plane and a Beaver landed, bringing the first of the flying guests.

Everyone had brought food (flown in on the planes) and I hardly lifted a finger to cook or peel a vegetable or wash a dish. German Nick is an excellent baker and he helped me produce multiple batches of bread. Songs were sung, plays were performed, and even the weather gods co-operated. Up until the Rainbows tour, the summer had been lousy, but it had cleared for that trip and stayed fabulous until the last guests left Nuk Tessli. On the 10th of August, the first batch of people flew out (twenty-five had stayed the previous night: a Nuk Tessli record) and Ellen arrived on their pickup plane. And yes, she had passed her shooting exam with flying colours—had, in fact, been dubbed the "small arms queen." A Leisure Islands Bus tour came from Victoria on the 11th, and on the 12th I took a group of party people to some meadows, which are usually at their peak at this time of year, on the flanks of the North Ridge. Because the plateau where we had camped on the hike in had been such a failure plantwise, I didn't know what to expect, but again the flower display was absolutely gorgeous.

Ellen and German Nick stayed on after everyone else had gone, but they could not delay indefinitely because Nick was working for a log builder in Germany and had limited vacation time, and Ellen would have to go back to school in the fall. They fitted in several hiking trips before they left; on their last one, they planned to climb Wilderness Mountain and check out

Mary's new cabin. I decided to hike up there to meet them so that I could make another effort at sorting out the trail.

Once again I slogged my way through the labyrinth of pools and ponds until I hit the river. To avoid the worst of the subalpine fir I climbed a little higher than I had done with Naomi, but ended up slopping through endless swamps. I would have to abandon the river route altogether if I couldn't find a better way through.

The morning had been sunny, but as I climbed higher a haze began to film the sky. And that presaged the end of our brief summer. At the cabin, the cloud thickened and the wind moaned, and by morning we were glad to bushwhack down into the shelter of the bush.

On top of the hundreds of hours of drudgery that Ellen performed when she first visited Nuk Tessli, she has left a special legacy to the place: she loves to sculpt wood. During the winter of 1998 she had whittled the head of an interesting little man with a frown on one side of his face and a sardonic grin on the other. This now sits on a bump on the curly post that supports the open end of the porch. At that time the stumps from the logging around the building site still stuck up above the snow and Ellen suggested that they, too, should all be carved. I thought that might look a bit too much like a theme park, but left a couple of them near the new wharf. Both curved about a metre high from the same rootstock.

Among the party visitors had been a woman called Julia Armstrong who had also worked a lot with wood. It was through Julia's family that I had met the Turners of Lonesome Lake and thus started my wilderness career. It was therefore appropriate that Julia should leave a little bit of herself behind at Nuk Tessli. She tackled the first of the stumps, and by the end of the day a wooden bear, his nose a natural protuberance in the tree trunk, stared somewhat bemusedly at the lake. Ellen chiselled the other stump into a leaping fish, its gaping mouth ready to snap at a mysterious something in the airspace above its head. These two manifestations of my friends' creativity are fitting guardians for my new home.

"Swiss chocolate, curries, Spotted Dick with golden syrup…"
Patricia Banning-Lover, Nuk Tessli guest book, 1993

2nd Oct 00

Dear Nick,

After concentrating for so long on the new cabin and getting ready for the party, there was the inevitable hiatus afterwards and it took a few days before I could summon up the energy to start anything constructive. I made a "do" list of thirty separate tasks. A lot of them were business chores, but the first outside job was to carve an owl's face on the back of Julia's bear. I hadn't realized how difficult it was to work with that green, resin-gobbed wood. Dry wood might be harder to cut but surely it is less messy to handle. Because of the fish's leaping pose and gaping mouth, I had thought that it would look as though it were about to eat the owl. But the owl has an earnest expression on his face and seems to be peering down the fish's mouth as if the fish were sitting in a dentist's chair! Every visitor has been very impressed with the sculptures, especially when I tell them they were carved by three different women.

Two days after you left, just as I was chopping onions for supper, a face framed by a backpack suddenly materialized by the kitchen window. As I was amazedly taking in the rain-shiny clothes and water-plastered hair, someone said: "It's the Germans." The only Germans that I knew in the neighbourhood were you guys, but you should have been arriving at Nimpo on that day. And behind the spokesman was another hiker...and another...and another...and another. Six in all. I was absolutely dumbfounded. A strange group arriving on foot

without warning has happened only once before in all the years I've been here. (The hikers said afterwards that the expression on my face was very comical.) It turned out that one of the men worked as a carpenter in Germany for the log builder who had made Mary's cabin, and who also exported houses over to Europe. The visitors had flown to Wilderness Lake intending to spend a couple of nights up there, then hike down to my place. Their first day was quite good weatherwise, windy but mostly sunny, so two of them had climbed Wilderness Mountain. From the summit, with binoculars, they could pick out the white canoe on its rack beside my cabins. They had no map but took a compass bearing on my place and figured it would not be too difficult to get there. They had never experienced untracked bush before.

Their trip, needless to say, was a nightmare. They were carrying far too much stuff—things like a bottle of wine they had not yet drunk—and the clouds were socked in so they could not see any landmarks. Not that they would have been able to see much anyway once they became embroiled in the Octopus Lake complex, and of course they didn't know about my existing trail coming down from the bridge either. So the poor souls bushwhacked all the way. After seven hours they arrived at my lake way up at the top end, even beyond where I had dragged Taya, but without a map, they didn't even know at first whether they had reached the right body of water. Fortunately they could just see a bit of Cabin One. The best choice of route for them at that point would have been to go upstream a short way until they could cross the river, then hike on the trail that runs along the north side of the lake. They would have been at my place within another forty minutes or so. But again they made the wrong decision and stayed on the south side. It took them a further two hours to reach the cabins. I decided, therefore, that once I caught up with the chores, I would turn my energies to working on the Wilderness Lake trail and its link to the existing trails around my lake.

Stuff for a couple of overnight camps was packed, and I was ready to go for over a week before the morning was calm enough to let me paddle up my lake without too much effort. Despite the excessively rainy summer, the country is now fairly dry. The Octopus Lakes are all very shallow and full of goose poop as Canada geese moult there during the summer; I didn't want to spend time boiling water for drinking, so I was extremely thirsty by the time I reached the river. It's not that I couldn't find the river, but I kept trying to work out the best way between one lake and the next, and simply went round in circles. First I worked without a pack and marked sections with flagging tape, then backtracked and picked up the ribbons when I realized I was getting nowhere. I didn't have very much flagging tape and what I had was yellowish green, not the best colour to use in a sun-dazzled forest. At one point we came upon a muddy hollow where much activity had recently taken place. It was obviously a bear wallow and a delighted Ginger promptly rolled in it.

In the end I picked up the pack and tried a route without ribboning, steering by the sun and what I could see of the mountains. I must have practically doubled back on myself, for after what seemed to be hours of walking I found myself at the river just before it enters that lake above Octopus Lake. After that I gave up and simply pushed upstream to Mary's cabin.

The six surprise Germans had seen a bear and five caribou during their one day up there, so I was not too surprised when Max took off during the late afternoon and tore across the outlet and up the other side of the lake. I caught a glimpse of a caribou but concentrated on grabbing Ginger, and in securing her I lost sight of the deer. Max ran all the way round to where he'd seen it and stayed quite a while sniffing round before he returned. Ginger, as you can imagine, was not well pleased.

I should have kept them both chained. Just on dusk, when I was already fishing their dog food out of their packs (and they were sitting eagerly in front of me: it's the only time they really love me), there was a clink of stone not far from the creek. The noise from the creek and the wind had obscured the animal's approach. Off tore the dogs. It was too dark for me to see the caribou, but through the binoculars I watched the pale form of

Max flit along the waterfront to about three-quarters of the way up the lake. Next thing, the large bull caribou jumped into the water. The lake still held the light from the evening sky and he was silhouetted against it. He had the most enormous rack I've ever seen. As he swam, his body sank; separated from his head by a section of water, his tail stuck up in the air like a periscope. Behind him two hornless animals leapt into the water, also with only their heads and tails showing—but no, these were not caribou, they were the dogs. Both of them. Ginger was actually swimming. All that angst about crossing the river had been a great big hoax. Yelling at the dogs was pointless; even if they had been inclined to come back, the strong wind would simply have carried my voice away. Ginger soon returned to shore, however, and after a while came back to the cabin alone. It was too dark to hunt for the dog chains without lighting a candle, and to make sure I knew where she was, I shut her inside. (The doors and windows had been put in just days before.)

The caribou was still swimming strongly. When Ginger had turned back, Max had faltered too and I thought he would give up, but when he saw the caribou still ahead of him, the temptation was too strong and he kept going. The distance between the animals did not vary, so they were obviously swimming at the same speed. When both of them were almost across the lake, Max finally quit. Slowly, slowly, I watched him go back across the choppy water, which must have been pretty cold. He had been swimming for a good twenty minutes by that time. At last he reached the shore close to where he had first plunged in. One would think that the caribou would be long gone by now, but not a bit of it. He had often turned his head to watch Max, and when the dog turned back, he also reversed his direction. So now the caribou was following the dog. Although I could see Max heave himself up onto the shore, he was out of view the moment he touched the rocks (it was now quite dark), but he must have stayed and watched the caribou, for he did not return to the cabin right away. The caribou was almost all the way back across the lake when he suddenly veered once more—he would have seen the dog again—and this time finally kept going to the other side. He would have been in the water for at least an hour by the time he climbed out. I have seen these animals crossing my lake sometimes; even the young ones are strong swimmers.

Excitement over, I opened the door of the cabin to retrieve Ginger, and got a shock. Ginger is a somewhat pungent dog at the best of times, and her brief immersion in the lake had brought out all her flavour. But her own smell was not the only thing to assail my olfactory senses. Added to the powerful redolence of wet dog was the even stronger aroma of wet bear gleaned from the wallow she had rolled in. I would not have thought that one small animal could have made so much stink.

8th Oct 00

Very warm, with an extremely erratic, gusty wind and a bit of spitty rain. But since I last wrote we had another short spell of cold but gorgeous weather, and off I went to Octopus Lake again. The thermometer on the tree registered 0°C. I've often suspected it to be inaccurate (it is an alcohol one: wouldn't the altitude affect it?) and it must have been quite a bit colder, for the ground was hard and a surprising amount of ice had formed in still places along the edge of the lake.

Coming down from Wilderness Lake the previous time, I had again gone round in circles, so I had come to the conclusion that the "shortcuts" around Octopus Lake were simply not going to work. After one more attempt I simply ribboned a trail more or less along the edge of the water but cutting off the worst of the convolutions. The map indicates that I have chosen quite a dog-leg for this route, but trying to make it straighter was obviously not going to work. The route at least has the advantage of several very pretty viewpoints. In fact it will be by far the most attractive hike in the area. The whole hike will probably take four or five hours when the trail is finished.

Marking a trail is not just a question of taking a swipe at a tree here and there along the route. Ideally one blaze should be visible from its neighbour, but often suitable trees are not available.

Because people are likely to be walking this trail without guides, I have filled the spaces between good blaze trees with cairns. The trees themselves at that elevation are slow growing so are very shrubby and branchy: many limbs needed to be cut off, some just so that I could reach the trunk with the axe to cut the blaze itself, and others well above and well below the mark so that twigs and shadows will not hide it. Ellen will be pleased to hear that my knuckles soon resembled hers when she was peeling logs.

Just above Octopus Lake is a very beautiful place along the river where the water widens into a calm sweep and a wide, grassy flat provides ample tenting spots. When the water is low a gravel bar provides an environmentally friendly place to build a fire, so this is where I made a camp. Looking upstream, the water and willows that fringe it—faded yellow and halfway leafless now—are backed by the ponderous grey peak at the north end of Flat Top Mountain. I built the fire while the last of the sun warmed me and a little sneaky wind blew chilly puffs downriver and batted smoke playfully into my face. I had a good blaze going and was warm enough but pulled on down coat and long johns, as I knew it would freeze the minute the sun went behind the mountain.

I used no tent for the camp, only the bivvy sack, so had an uninterrupted view of the stars and satellites and an energetic display of northern lights. They had been playing for about four nights in a row at that point. The dogs were supremely disgusted, but they were tied for the night. The morning produced another thick, white frost and the cold extruded those peculiar ice "shavings" that often happen under these conditions all over the gravel bar. Each of the faded yellow willow leaves was etched with ice and a tiny, calm inlet tucked in behind the gravel bar was frozen over. As the sun rose, grey puffs of mist grew larger and swallowed the world. It was very quiet and grey and soft and beautiful. All of a sudden it must have grown a fraction warmer, for I was aware of small movements all over the gravel bar where the ice "shavings" were collapsing, causing the little pebbles to shift and settle as they did so.

By the time the day was finished, all but a short strip of the trail was blazed. The uncompleted section bypassed some pretty obvious landmarks, so I figured that if I didn't get up there again this year and the flagging tape was destroyed by the elements, I could still find the route in the spring. These landmarks are two groups of quite large ponds, the first of them just past the basin skirted by the trail to the Octopus Lake Bridge (which is where the two trails now diverge). I have often skied over these ponds in winter but did not know what was underneath the snow—water, swamp or tundra. Well, the first group of ponds has permanent water and swamp, but the second group at present is bone dry. It is a kettle pond, of which there are a number in that area. Kettle ponds are formed when glaciers bury huge lumps of ice beneath the gravel that they leave. As they recede, the surface is scraped flat, but when the buried ice eventually melts, a depression is formed. It fills with water in the spring but has no inlet and has usually evaporated by the end of summer. These particular kettle ponds are the largest I've seen around here. Judging by the rotten logs washed up around the rim, they must sometimes fill completely, but the species of vegetation among the stones round the edge indicates they either dry quickly or the snowmelt no longer fills them. It will be interesting to check them out in the spring. Through the middle of the pond, in the direction I want to go, are several large erratics (boulders dropped by the glacier) and I have placed cairns on top of these as markers. It's going to look pretty funny when the pond is full of water. I remember a wild river in New Zealand that had an outcrop of rock in the middle of it, and someone—somehow—had placed a McDonald's golden arches sign on top with "just 5 mins away" written on it. (This was when McDonald's had just been introduced to New Zealand.) I don't think I will go quite that far, though. Somehow I don't think "Bear Tooth Bakery: Just 2 hours away" will have the right ring. Or how about: "Chris's Famous Stone Oven Pizza"...?

The weather stayed good a couple of days after the camp trip so once again I canoed round the lake and hiked up to the top of

"Kettle Pond Flat." I packed the clippers as well as the axe, as I intended to start on the brushing. There was still a good frost, but as I climbed up the steep slope from the lakeshore my nose registered occasional eddies of warm air and hazy streaks of cloud began to curl about the sky, so obviously a change was coming. At the confluence of the trails I stopped for a snack and one or two blackflies made their presence felt.

The final stretch of trail was easy to blaze and I brushed as I went. Brushing is no more straightforward than blazing. The eye has to move along the trail as easily as the feet. Ends of branches that divert vision from the trail, even if they are not actually in the way, must be cleared out. If I had fifty people following me, none of my elaborate marking would be necessary. Or, better still, twenty horses. Once it is worn into the ground, the trail will be there forever, but until the mark on the ground is made, the other signs must be as clear as possible.

By midday I had finished the unblazed piece. But so much for my plans of continuing the brushing, for working up there was an absolute torment. The blackflies were like nothing I have ever experienced. They crawled into my ears and up my nose and into the corners of my eyes. I was tossing and shaking my head like a horse. I lathered on bug dope with the consequence that my nose and eyes ran copiously—that stuff makes me sneeze—but it didn't seem to make much difference to the flies. So although it seemed a real waste of effort quitting so early, I had to give up. When I walked at normal speed, the flies were not so noticeable. My lake was dead calm; I was expecting to be mobbed so didn't stop to admire the view but jumped straight into the canoe and paddled home, cursing the fact that I'd already taken down the screen door. But at home there were hardly any flies. Why they should be so horrendous 100 m higher, goodness only knows. Blackflies breed in running water and on Kettle Pond Flat there is none; in fact there is no surface water at all right now. If the weather turns good again I'll spend another night or two up there—it is so incredibly pretty—but I'll want a good frost before I do.

22nd Oct 00

We've had huge dumps of rain and snow; this has to be the wettest fall on record. Even as I write, the sun is dissolving in a grey wall of vapour that is climbing high into the sky and making Monarch look pretty sick, so it probably won't be long before it is snowing again. Round the cabin the temperature has been around or just above freezing, so snow accumulation is only a few centimetres, but Louise O'Murphy is blinding, thickly white; it must be pretty deep up there.

Before the snow, however, the weather was beautiful. We finally had about ten days of summer. Made up for the winter we had in July, I guess. I didn't get up to Octopus Lake, but worked on the trail around the south shore of my lake. You will be amazed when you see it: it is not just a trail, it's a freeway. It's not quite finished yet—I had just ribboned the last stretch, the section between the river and the end of the existing trail at "Sunrise Viewpoint," when this last lot of snow started and I didn't fancy whacking away at trees while gobs of snow fell down my neck.

Most mornings it was freezing quite hard and consequently chilly on that shady side of the lake. But as soon as it warmed up enough to stop nipping my toes, the blackflies fell upon me with great joy. So most times, although I took a lunch, I didn't work all that late. I shall be leaving for the outside again in a few days, so now that this snow has come, it looks as though the rest of the trail will have to wait until next year.

Love
Chris

*"Sitting here in your fabulous guest cabin and full
of Spotless Dick, I'm grateful to be here..."*
—Paul Vanpeenen, Nuk Tessli guest book, 1997
(That was the time I had no raisins.)

1st Jan 01

Dear Nick,

Last year was a low-snow winter, but this year is even worse
and has beaten all records. Usually there is at least half a metre
around the cabins by Christmas but this year there are barely 15
cm and patches of ground in the windy places are bare. When I
flew in a week ago, I did not even need the snowshoes to get up
to my cabin.

My time outside was not as lucrative as it has been on other
occasions and my financial problems, which have been looking
worse as the year progressed, have escalated into horrendous
proportions.

The tourist income for the year 2000 was poor. I lost custom
both due to the bad weather (two parties were delayed and one
of the bus tours couldn't land) and because of a horrible plane
crash in the area last spring that seriously injured three people

and killed three others. It made TV news and two more parties cancelled because of it, even though the man who piloted the crashed plane never brought people in to my place and will never fly anywhere again. Add that to the fact that bookings were fewer than normal in the first place, and you will see why it has been my poorest year to date.

My book income has received some pretty hard knocks as well. In the fall, I heard that *Diary of a Wilderness Dweller*, which has been my best seller, is suddenly out of print. It will be issued again at some point—it's too good to abandon entirely—but that doesn't help me now. Stock of *Cabin at Singing River* is also getting very low. I now own the publishing rights to that and I certainly won't be able to reprint it until my finances improve. Added to which, the royalties for *Nuk Tessli: The Life of a Wilderness Dweller*, which I was relying upon to cover a number of bills, were non-existent last year. This was partly because of a merger by two major book companies that resulted in the closure of several large bookstores. When a bookseller buys from a publisher he has to pay within a certain time but reserves the option to return the books if they are not sold. These are called buy-backs and are usually so few as to be insignificant. But the store closures meant that a great wave of books was returned to the publishers, who suffered greatly as a result, and one major distributor simply collapsed, throwing everyone further into hardship. The authors had to pay back their royalties and I have ended up owing the publisher money instead of the other way round. Since I have lived in the wilderness my finances have always been very precarious and I've never been able to save a dime. When something like this happens I have no resources to fall back on.

But I might have been able to scrape through if the Land Office hadn't also chosen this year to ding me with a 600% increase in fees. They said they were restructuring their back-country recreation policy and, although I had a current agreement that was supposed to run for several more years, they blithely cancelled that (because they are the government they are not obliged to follow normal business rules) and made me apply for a new one—complete with the several hundred dollars' worth of application fees that this entails. Last fall I was able to point out a gross error in one of their figures when their bill was exorbitantly high. I am supposed to pay a head tax of a dollar per person-day if I entertain more than 500 people-days per annum. Even including the bus tours I've never processed more than 500 here. The bill last fall was, however, for 3,000 people/days. Instead of my tourist numbers, they had looked at my gross income, which for that year was $3,000!)

Up until now, my rent has been $630 per year, payable in November. Last August I was presented with another bill for over

$5,000, to be Paid By September The Fifteenth Or Else. The people-day error had been corrected, but they had managed to put in another one. They had backdated the bill for two years to the time when they forced me to apply for a new licence—even though they continued to charge for the old one, which was supposed to be defunct! This is the third major billing error the Land Office has made since I have dealt with them. Extra to this, the $1,000 safekeeping bond I already have with a bank had to be increased to $2,500. I decided that was within my means so sent off the forms and a cheque for the difference: $1,500. Then of course I get a letter back from the bank (a month later) telling me they cannot just increase the bond. I have to present the bank with $2,500, upon which they will return the $1,000. What stupid kind of rule is that? As I was still in the bush at the time and did not have $2,500, I could not do this by mail and so wrote to both the Land Office and the bank, telling them that everything would have to wait until I went out at the end of October. Fortunately, although the Land Office documents are worded in an extremely threatening manner, I have found the personnel to be quite reasonable when I actually contact them face to face. I had a few slide shows in November and ended up scraping together all the funds that were required for the Land Office, but at the expense of other bills. The publisher cannot be paid and I now owe Mary two years' rent for the Nimpo cabin. She has been very understanding about that. If only there was some way of paying this off it wouldn't be so bad, but at the moment the future looks very gloomy.

I tried to get a job for the winter, but although I can do so many things, I am in fact virtually unemployable. My body won't allow me to do heavy physical work like tree planting or peeling logs any more; my carpentry standards aren't good enough for anything but the roughest work; I can type and use my ancient Mac Classic but know nothing about handling computers or any kind of office work; I'm not good with kids, can't imagine I'd be able to manage waitressing and don't have the personality (or the clothes!) to work in a store. I would go completely bananas saying "Have a nice day" at the checkout counter. I'd be a good house painter or gardener, but neither of those jobs is available in the winter, and although I asked everyone I could think of and a few said they might have something, employment never happened.

Consequently, I figured I might just as well go home. Because fewer people came during the summer than expected I still had a lot of dried and canned food stored there and even with the cost of the plane flights it would be cheaper to spend the next three months at Nuk Tessli. It would certainly keep me a lot saner. Besides, after such a long stint of art-deprived existence I was dying to work on another book. A failure to be published does not halt the driving urge to be creative. Two years of letter writing to you has certainly provided me with enough material. What do you think of *Spotted Dick* for a title?

On my way home from the outside world I reached Williams Lake on the 19th of December. From Emily's I called Mary to see if she had any free-range eggs; if not I would pick up my winter's supply in town. "Where are you?" she said as soon as she heard my voice. "We need you."

And this is what she told me.

Stanley Edwards, the cheerful old fellow we canoed up the Stillwater to visit when you were here in '98, had been found dead in the bush. When I called his sister Trudy to give my condolences, she told me he had been fine on the 1st of December when she had driven him up the Tote Road at the bottom of The Hill, but he did not turn up when expected, two weeks later, to the room he has kept for a number of years at one of the valley hotels. The hotel owner phoned the police, who apparently informed him that they couldn't go looking for anyone who simply failed to arrive for his dinner. Stanley, however, was always pretty reliable about coming out on time, so the hotel owner dispatched two guys to look for him. There was not much snow and they were able to drive along the Tote Road. They didn't have to hike up to Stanley's place, however, because he was at the tiny cabin the linemen camped in when the telegraph used to operate through there. The poor fellow was sitting in the outhouse, frozen stiff. His sleeping bag was laid out in the cabin, so he had presumably been on his way out. The police then went in and fetched him, and finally Trudy was notified. Stanley had apparently suffered a heart attack. Trudy began to make funeral arrangements but their brother John wanted to see Stanley before he was shipped to Williams Lake for cremation. The only trouble was, John was up at his parents' old homestead at Lonesome Lake. Nimpo Nick offered to fly in and fetch him, but it had been a very mild fall and the ice was not good enough for a plane to land on; also, John could not leave without someone there to keep his fires stoked, otherwise his home-canned vegetables would freeze.

As planes could not be used to fetch John, a man called Merrit Sager, who lives north of Anahim, was persuaded to take his helicopter in. Various people around Nimpo might have been willing to house-sit for John, but it was already the 19th of December and the weather was very unstable: no one wanted to risk getting stuck in there over Christmas. I didn't want to go either—not because of missing Christmas (I had expected to spend it at home alone, anyway) but because I dread flying. Now I would have to psych myself up for three flights instead of one before I could get home. But all the Edwards family, Trudy,

Stanley and John, were good neighbours to me when I lived at Lonesome Lake and it was the least I could do. Besides, I had not been back to my old cabin since I had left it fourteen years before and I was curious to see how it had survived.

I arrived at Nimpo well after dark on the 20th of December. I phoned the chopper pilot and he said there was very little passenger space, so there would be no room for the dogs. Mary said she would look after them. I warned her not to let them off and not to lead-walk them, as they would pull her off her feet. It wouldn't be much fun for them but if all went well it would be for only two nights. Should the weather deteriorate further and leave me stranded, there would be enough strong guys around over Christmas to give them some exercise.

Merrit had a logging machinery crisis and could not fly on the 21st, and in any case the weather was very dark and gloomy. On the 22nd it was marginally better and calm. Low cloud lopped off the tops of all the mountains: no one could have got into my place, but Lonesome Lake is a lot lower than Nimpo and John said the ceiling was 1,500 m a.g.l. down there.

Aware of my dislike of flying, Merrit took off very gently. Apparently if they whiz off as they do in the movies, you feel as though you are going to free-fall into space. It was such a calm day there was no turbulence and we seemed to move very slowly over the ranchland and Anahim Lake; in fact this particular machine travels quite a bit slower than a Cessna 180. And I almost enjoyed it. My difficulty with flying is not fear of crashing or of heights, the kind of things that bedevil most people, but claustrophobia—I'm trapped in there and can't get out. The chopper's cab was a great bubble, with glass even below my feet, and being so close to the trees, I felt I could simply open the door and step through.

We headed for a tiny V on the horizon just visible below the great grey lid of cloud. The gap marked the head of the Precipice Valley, where Dave and Rosemary Neads live. Although I've been down there a couple of times, I have never seen the upper part of the canyon, which is away from the road and the homesteads. The beginning of this great gouge in the landscape is very dramatic. The comparatively flat plateau is suddenly cleaved by this giant trough, the top of which is rimmed by basalt cliffs. Many of the hexagonal columns are twisted and buckled, and the convolutions of the rock were starkly emphasized as all the ribs were etched with snow. We dropped down into the valley and suddenly there were Lee Taylor's cows, fat black ants on the little white cloth of the meadow. We flew directly over Dave and Rosemary's house; I had spoken to Rosemary on the phone, so they would know exactly why the helicopter was chugging along over their heads. Then came Jim Glenn's place, and finally the plunge through the deep part of the canyon. There is what looks like soft shale made from volcanic ash at the bottom of the magma, and at one point the river cascaded into a classic sink-hole. I must walk that canyon sometime: I bet there are fossils to die for down there.

The canyon connected with the Atnarko Valley at the head of the Tote Road where Lonesome Lake residents have always left their vehicles when travelling back and forth. The lineman's shack, where Stanley was found, was a couple of kilometres north toward the highway. The 5 km of trail we walked two years ago between the Tote Road and the Stillwater was invisible from the air as it was buried beneath the forest canopy; the distance was covered in an instant in the chopper. The lake was frozen over except for the black, winding snake of the river channel, which was dotted with a few white and grey trumpeter swans. I couldn't see anything of Stanley's buildings, but of course thought of him and his wheelbarrow roads as we flew overhead. As we trundled past Hunlen Canyon I got a glimpse of the falls swathed in ice, and then we were over Lonesome Lake with its strange and interesting patterns of black leads on the greyish sur-face. I've skied down Lonesome Lake at Christmastime before but I sure wouldn't have wanted to use the ice right then. In one spot there was what looked like an immense single tire track with a few dots at one end. It must have been where a swan had taken off and beaten the dusting of snow with its huge wings for about

30 m before he managed to get into the air. Swans like to sit out on thin ice, as they feel safe from predators.

At the head of the lake were the old homestead buildings with the tiny, foreshortened figure of John at the door, his orange wool hat the only speck of colour in a landscape of whites and greys. John had stamped out a landing pad with snowshoes and laid two timbers across it so the chopper skids would not sink. Rain had fallen since the snow had accumulated (there was a lot more there than at Nimpo), so there was not a lot of powder blown about when the chopper landed.

John took about twenty minutes to describe how he wanted his two stoves stoked and various other chores done, mostly regarding the feeding of his neighbourhood fox and martens. He had told me earlier on the radiophone that he had counted twenty-four martens the year before and was obtaining all kinds of interesting data. He said he could fill thirteen encyclopoedias with what he had learned.

John's lifelong dream has been to restore the old homestead, and he had done a great deal of work since I was last in the valley. The main room of the house was still dark and full of books and cardboard cartons with tiny alleys in between. Most of John's and his parents' possessions are stored there. The kitchen had more windows and was lighter, as he was in the process of lining the walls and ceiling and painting them white. With two stoves going, the house was toasty warm. All the Edwardses were great readers so there was no lack of material to keep me entertained.

John had snowshoes I could borrow, so the following day I trudged the 4 km upriver to my old cabin. It was fairly hard work breaking trail, but I've known worse. The weather had improved: it was almost sunny on occasion. Tramping the trails that were at one time so familiar, but that I had not seen for fourteen years, I expected to feel something: excitement? déjà vu? But nothing much happened until I entered the fence that marked Trudy and Jack's claim, and passed the place where I had camped while building my cabin. Then I had a sudden strong awareness, not of the Turners or myself, but of my old dog Lonesome. Perhaps I was missing my own dogs; perhaps I had been thinking of Lonesome because of working on her manuscript on and off throughout the year. Who knows? But the sense of her was so strong that I kept looking for her, even though my brain told me she could not possibly be there. It was quite disconcerting.

The cabin looked in pretty good shape considering I had removed the windows and the chimney when I left. That the roof was still on surprised me, for I didn't think I had built it all that well. Very little snow had blown in through the empty window holes, but a cone of snow was piled below the chimney. I had put an old pot up there but it must have blown off. There was still quite a pile of firewood in the woodshed.

Cabin at Lonesome Lake

The only thing I had really regretted leaving behind when I moved to Nuk Tessli were the chainsaw-milled boards. I had made 1,300 of them all told, all out of Douglas fir. I had thought of them often as I struggled to make more lumber up at Nuk Tessli. Now a couple of floorboards were missing and I assumed the Turners had used them for something before they moved out, but John later told me he had taken one of them to make a guide board for his own lumber making. He has sawn a huge pile of beautiful cedar to use in the restoration of his homestead. This, I felt, was apt because when I first started lumber making and needed a guide board, there was none to be had. The Turners had used split cedar slabs for all their structures that weren't built of logs and there wasn't a sawn board on the place. But one day

I found a rotten plank washed up at the edge of the lake. It would have come from the old homestead's water-driven sawmill. I had backpacked it up the river to start off my own lumber making; now the favour had been returned.

The 24th was a beautiful sunny morning and John must have set off early from Bella Coola, for the chopper was in by about 10 a.m. It was a breathless day to be flying. Merrit took me right into the Hunlen Falls canyon. The spray always freezes around waterfalls, eventually enclosing the falling water entirely. The 300 m drop was encased in a solid column of greenish ice. Through it, the water could be glimpsed on its endless tumble, down, down, it seemed from our mosquito-eye view, to the bottom of the world.

At Nimpo, I was informed that Floyd, my usual pilot, was away but a man called Buddy Jones would be happy to fly me home. Remember Buddy? He used to own the resort on Charlotte Lake at the mouth of Whitton Creek. When Lonesome (dog) and I had that adventure with the bear climbing into the trap cabin, she, brave soul, ran away and ended up at his place.* Buddy is a marine pilot and therefore away a lot and his wife did not want to live alone in a roadless place in the bush, so they sold the resort and built a house at Nimpo.

* See *Diary of a Wilderness Dweller.*

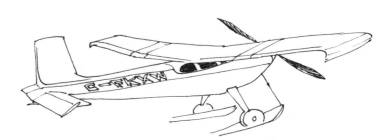

The Gold-Plated Aeroplane

A few years ago, Buddy refurbished his plane, a Cessna 180. It has real leather upholstery, carpets in the luggage compartment, and (you'll never believe this!) gold-plated fittings. Apparently Buddy wanted chrome on the metal parts, such as window hinges, but the guy who was going to do it said he had a new gold-plating machine he wanted to try out and he gave Buddy a deal. So me and my scruffy hounds were flown home in a gold-plated airplane!

All the very best for the coming year,

Love
Chris

SPOTTED DICK

My memory may be playing tricks, but it seems to me I ate Spotted Dick at least twice a week when I was growing up. My mother would cut out a quarter and divide that between me, my brother and herself. My dad would be offered the rest; what he didn't eat my brother and I would consume the next day after school, fried, with golden syrup poured on top of it.

The spotted dick I remember is a steamed pudding made with white flour, suet,* lard, salt, baking powder and water, and traditionally "spotted" with currants. It was always served with hot custard sauce made from Birds Instant Custard Powder.

A recipe adapted from *The American Woman's Cook Book*, edited by Ruth Berolzheimer (1958), goes as follows.

1 cup raisins	3 cups sifted flour
1 cup ground suet*	1 tsp baking powder
1 tsp salt	1 cup liquid (milk, sour milk or water)

*Suet is kidney fat ground into wheat-sized pieces. When I was a child it could be bought from the butcher or from a grocery store in cardboard boxes.

Mix dry ingredients. Add liquid and mix thoroughly: the batter should be sticky but not sloppy. Fill a greased pudding mould two-thirds full. Cover tightly and steam 3 hours. Serves 8 to 10 (or 3 hungry young Germans.)

I steam it by putting the dough into a handle-less pot with a plate over the top (curved side up, or the condensation runs inside) and placing the whole in a large stockpot with water in the bottom. Some kind of rack (I use three canning jar lids) should separate the two containers. Ms. Berolzheimer advocates steaming for three hours but I find one hour is usually sufficient for a pudding of that size (a larger one may take longer). I often double my recipe: it is good cold, and it warms particularly well in a microwave.

For various reasons, including availability of ingredients and preference, I have modified Ms. Berolzheimer's recipe.

Spotted Dick à la Nuk Tessli

Start with the recipe above, but:

- I use whole wheat flour instead of white. It makes a heavier pudding but improves the flavour.
- I use raisins most of the time but any tart fruit, such as cut-up apricots, rhubarb or fresh wild huckleberries, can be substituted.

- I use about half the fat. Suet is not often available so I chop lard and rub it into the flour, as for pastry. Vegetable oil is a poor substitute; it makes a rubbery pudding. I have not tried butter but I imagine it would work very well. I should think the pudding would be pretty heavy without any fat at all.
- Eggs make it lighter and richer.
- I never use sweetener in the dough.
- Sunflower or sesame seeds add an interesting flavour.
- The custard sauce is made according to the directions on the Birds Instant Custard Powder can. As I have no liquid milk I add powdered milk with the other dry ingredients and use water for the liquid. (A tip for using powdered milk in any custard-style puddings, homemade yogurt, etc.: if you use the amount of milk powder called for on the packet, the pudding will not thicken or set properly. Toss in extra milk powder, up to half again as much. A good way of getting extra vitamin B and calcium.)

The Nuk Tessli Secret

After pouring the custard onto the portion of pudding on your plate, add maple syrup and home-canned huckleberries (processed without sugar). The secret is to have the three separate tastes: the bland, dumpling-like pudding, the sweet sauce and the very tart fruit.

ENJOY!

Stone Ovens and Stone Oven Bread

Since this book was written, I have built four more stone ovens, all for friends, and learned quite a bit more about them. For those who wish to experiment with stone oven building, here is a little more information.

1. The best rock for this purpose is soapstone, but it is very expensive and hard for most people to get. A good second choice is granite. I have built two limestone ovens, which did not seem as efficient, but I used each of them only once. Both my own ovens needed a couple of tries before I got used to their idiosyncrasies.

2. The roof should be about 45 cm above the flow of the oven. Any lower and the fire does not have enough room to generate sufficient heat.

3. The efficiency of the oven is vastly improved by throwing dirt over the top to seal the cracks and add bulk. But care must be taken to leave enough space at the back for a thorough draft, otherwise the back of the oven won't heat.

4. Once the ashes have been raked out, slop the floor with a wet mop. It really cleans the baking stove—and the steam is gratifyingly dramatic!

ACKNOWLEDGEMENTS

lthough I write my books on a computer, I cannot yet afford a satellite connection, which is the only type of phone that would enable me to link Nuk Tessli with either an ordinary telephone network or the Internet. Consequently I am reliant on a number of people to assist me when communicating with the outside world.

Firstly, Mary Kirner, owner of my "townhouse" (a cabin at the Nimpo Lake Resort that I use as an outside base) and the best landlady anyone could wish for; Mary also collects my mail, monitors the radiophone and organizes freighting of emergency supplies when necessary. She spends much time and energy assisting friends, some of whom don't speak much English, who arrive on her doorstep without the faintest idea of how they are going to take that final incomprehensible jump from the familiar road to my wilderness door.

Secondly, thanks to Rosemary Neads, who handles all my email inquiries with great finesse and charm; without her, publishers would be tearing their hair, my web site would be pointless and my ecotourism business would grind to a halt.

In the Lower Mainland and Vancouver Island I must thank Elizabeth and Alan Bell, and Corry Lunn and Darrel Nygaard, for holding my country bumpkin hand in the city and providing havens for extended periods of time while I have either done business down there, or taken jobs in their neighbourhoods when I was sorely in need of extra cash. Emily Patinaude and Blair Smith provide a similarly unconditional welcome in Williams Lake.

I must also thank local pilots, notably Floyd Vaughn, Nick Christianson, Buddy Jones and Warren Bean, for flying me and dogs and other awkward loads at all sorts of times not necessarily convenient to themselves. Finally, I wish to thank John Kerr, the Chilcotin's computer guru, and Rory Wickes and Dianne Chamberlain of the Anahim Lake School, who pooled skills, equipment and time to translate the ancient Mac programs in which this book was written into an electronic form that the publisher could read, all in the last two days before school closed for Christmas.

I might refer to myself as a Wilderness Dweller, but with these people supporting me, I will never be remote or isolated. Thank you one and all.

INDEX